**Schlumberger Cambridge
Research Centre**

Phaidon Press Limited
140 Kensington Church Street
London W8 4BN

First published 1993

© 1993, Phaidon Press Limited
Photographs © copyright 1993,
Dennis Gilbert except where stated to
the contrary

ISBN 0 7148 2774 6

A CIP catalogue record for this book
is available from the British Library

All rights reserved. No part of this
publication may be reproduced, stored
in a retrieval system, or transmitted in
any form or by any means, electronic,
mechanical, photocopying, recording
or otherwise, without the prior
permission of Phaidon Press Limited.

Acknowledgements: the author would
like to thank John Pringle of Michael
Hopkins and Partners for his help in
mining the office archive and for
scrutinizing the drawings. Thanks are
also due to Brian Forster of Ove Arup
& Partners for assisting with archive
research, to Anthony Hunt for allowing
his original sketches to be published,
and to Andrew Meade for photographic
research. Photograph no. 6 is by
Richard Einzig; no. 11 is by Martin
Charles; no. 22 is by Richard Bryant;
no. 45 is by Pat Hunt. All other material
except where stated is reproduced by
courtesy of Michael Hopkins and
Partners, London.

Printed in Singapore

Schlumberger Cambridge Research Centre
Michael Hopkins and Partners

David Jenkins
ARCHITECTURE IN DETAIL

Architecture at the cutting edge

Schlumberger is one of the world's great technological companies. From its foundation in 1927 by two French brothers, Conrad and Marcel Schlumberger, the company has operated at the frontiers of scientific advance; the brothers pioneered the use of surface electrical 'logging' to investigate the subsurface of the earth, leaving behind the old method of taking drill cuttings and core samples. Today, Schlumberger leads the world in the provision of oilfield technical services, maintaining its position in the vanguard through constant research into all aspects of hydrocarbon well drilling and production.

Michael Hopkins and Partners' Schlumberger Cambridge Research Centre plays a key role in this arena. Hopkins' original exuberant High-tech pavilion, completed in 1985, 1, supports Schlumberger's current programme of investigation into drilling and fluid mechanics, rock and wellbore physics, and the computer modelling of drilling information. Hopkins' new reception building, opened in 1992, provides additional facilities for seismic and rheological research. Schlumberger's programme involves a multi-disciplinary team of scientists whose activities are centred around the industry's most advanced drilling test station. The test rigs here are backed up with sophisticated control and data logging instrumentation, enabling the centre to provide critical intelligence which is applied in the field via the research and engineering centres of Schlumberger's world-wide operating companies.

In company with fellow industrial giants like Cummins, Herman Miller and IBM, Schlumberger's progressive attitude is reflected in its patronage of innovative architecture. Alongside Michael Hopkins' appointment at Cambridge, the company's recent roll of honour includes Philip Johnson and Howard Barnstone who designed research facilities at Ridgefield, Connecticut USA in the 1970s and Renzo Piano, who completed a major refit of Schlumberger's Paris headquarters in 1983. Hopkins himself was first commissioned in 1982 after rising to the top of a shortlist of twenty international practices.

A question of location

Finding a site for the company became a joint venture between architect and client. Schlumberger was looking for a location close to an existing centre of research expertise. The Hopkins office investigated a number of possibilities around Cambridge before recommending a 7 hectare plot in the High Cross Research Park. It has the advantages of close proximity to Cambridge city centre and to the M11 and thus easy access to London. It forms part of a designated science park on land owned by the university and, at the time Schlumberger made its decision, was already home to

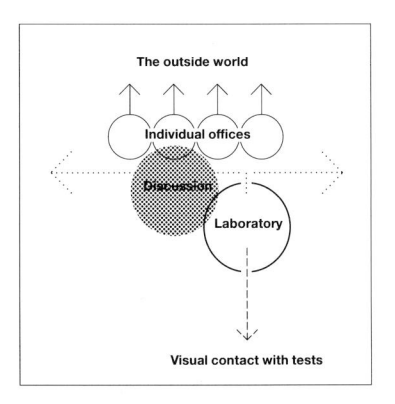

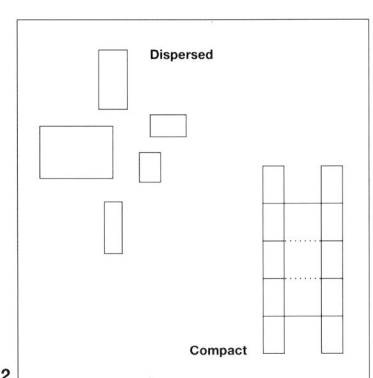

1 Hopkins' Schlumberger ensemble comprises the rigged and tented test station building, completed in 1985; and its more modest counterpart, the reception building, opened in 1992.

2 Hopkins' early exploration of Schlumberger's programme included a diagrammatic analysis of interdepartmental relationships and the arrangement of individual building elements on the site.

two prominent research establishments, a school of vetinary medicine and the British Antarctic Survey.

The brief that Schlumberger gave Hopkins for the test station building articulated a requirement for the maximum physical and visual cross-contact between the centre's constituent departments; for example, between theoretical and experimental research staff, scientists and administrators, recreation and work-places and large and small scale spaces. It also emphasized the need for flexible facilities for inter-departmental meetings and conferences with visiting university scientists or staff from other Schlumberger companies, encouraging further cross-contact between those in the building and the world outside, **2**.

As part of the initial familiarization process that followed his appointment, Michael Hopkins and project architect John Pringle visited Schlumberger's sister facility, the Schlumberger-Doll Research Center at Ridgefield, which satisfies a similar programme, to judge the company's design and environmental standards at first hand.

Hopkins' preliminary design report, presented to Schlumberger in April 1982, investigated a variety of linear, deep plan and courtyard configurations for the new building. The realized scheme might be thought of as a pioneering hybrid of all three types. It incorporates linear accommodation wings and central enclosed courtyard spaces which are combined to allow flexible movement patterns through what becomes a 50m deep, H-block, plan in which all the centre's activities are on display.

This begins to sound like a recipe for chaos, but the display is made coherent by the fact that Hopkins appoints each element of the programme with a specific spatial condition: individual outward-looking rooms for private study; open discussion areas and wide circulation routes, **3**, for *ad hoc* meetings; inward-facing laboratories for each scientific department; central, fabric-roofed, spaces for the test station – which gives the building its research focus – and for the 'winter garden' which now performs as restaurant and social gathering place. Within this community, each department is encouraged to form its own clear identity whilst relating to the centre as a whole.

Transparency and adjacency

Entering the winter garden via the open-air path that leads from the reception building, the visitor is presented with a narrative of the building in action. Behind the great glass wall ahead, **4**, is the experimental forum of the test station; its remarkable machinery and industrial toughness placed in marked juxtaposition with the planted and welcoming winter garden. In the distance, just discernible through the station's glazed end wall, is the rawness of the service yard

3 Open areas for informal meetings and discussion are provided in the test station building by widening the circulation routes at strategic crossing points.

4 The experimental forum of the test station is divided from the social arena of the winter garden by a great glass wall which allows clear views along the length of the building.

with its murky balancing pond and storage tanks. Changing focus, the story continues in the wings, with glimpses of the quiet activity in the laboratories and the scientists' rooms beyond.

The transparency which makes this reading so straightforward, and daytime working so pleasurable, turns the building at night into a piece of light-industrial theatre, **5**; all of which results from Hopkins' manipulation of the programme, creating an integrated building from what, in other circumstances, might have been a series of discrete pavilions. In this light, Schlumberger can be seen as evidence of Hopkins' continuing preoccupation with both literal transparency and social integration that has its beginnings in his early days of partnership with Norman Foster.

Foster Associates' IBM Pilot Head Office building at Cosham, 1970–71, is largely Michael Hopkins' work, **6**. Like Schlumberger it is a symmetrical building whose axis is used as a compositional, but not a communicational, device. It is also transparent, the long views through its glazed perimeter corresponding with the cross-axial circulation routes. IBM, Cosham, combines a multiplicity of functions and aims directly at a high degree of social integration; a large, highly-serviced computer room, a restaurant and lavatory blocks are brought together beneath a single 'umbrella' roof alongside cellular and open-plan offices, **7**.

The glass-fronted individual offices are placed back-to-back between the circulation 'lanes' that lead from the spinal 'street', forcing the company's managers to filter through the open-plan secretarial and administrative areas to reach their desks. Hopkins' and Foster's egalitarianism encourages the erosion of old-fashioned hierarchical barriers and, incidentally, gives the junior staff the best view of the surrounding countryside. The social principles established at IBM informed many later Foster projects, most notably, office buildings for Willis Faber Dumas in Ipswich, and the Hongkong and Shanghai Bank.[1]

During Hopkins' period in the office, Foster Associates also progressed the idea of reconciling the apparently irreconcilable within a single building envelope with a project for the German Car Centre at Milton Keynes, 1972–74. Here the oppositions of quiet/noisy, clean/dirty, high space/low space were brought together, uniting car servicing and body-work repair shops, parts warehousing and open-plan offices beneath a single rectilinear roof. The issues of adjacency were resolved technically and formally, but fundamentally were pursued in the interests of a better workplace.[2]

Flexibility and expansion

Tracing this thinking back to its source, one finds the infinitely flexible serviced umbrella structures of Ezra Ehrenkrantz's

5 At night the test station building becomes transparent, its curious pupae-like forms glowing on the skyline.
6, 7 IBM Cosham, a project in which Michael Hopkins was closely involved while in partnership with Sir Norman Foster. It is a precursor of Schlumberger's egalitarian approach to workplace design.

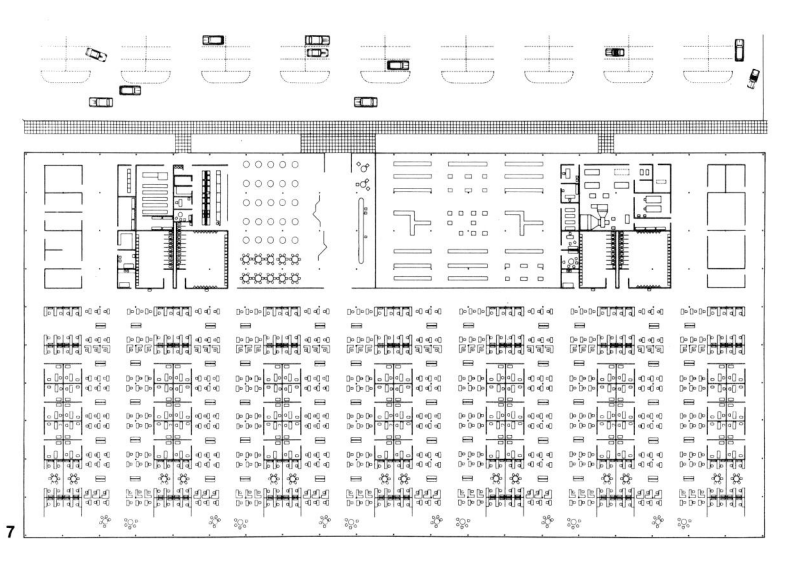

Californian School Construction Systems Development (SCSD) programme of the early 1960s. Both Hopkins and Foster drew inspiration from Ehrenkrantz's work. In fact their partnership led ultimately from a chance meeting at an Architectural Association crit at which Patty Hopkins presented, as a thesis project, a health centre based on the SCSD system.³

Although it represents an obvious formal departure from the SCSD and early Foster models, to a degree, Schlumberger incorporates the notions of flexibility that Ehrenkrantz advocated. It is a responsive structure with an adaptable, but discreet, services network designed to follow the future arrangement of the office and laboratory wings as the client's requirements alter and evolve.

The building is also deliberately open-ended, allowing the possibility of modular expansion in either direction. The initial intention was to construct the scheme in two or more phases, **8**. The first phase of 5600m² is as we see the test station building now. A further linear phase was intended to add extra office, laboratory and conference space at the southern end of the building, bringing the total floor area up to 8000m².

Paradoxically, Hopkins' new extension takes up few of the original building's structural and organizational clues. Denied the programmatic thrust of a test station or winter garden, it is conceived instead as a free-standing reception building, situated in front of the original winter garden terrace. Formally, the new building can be seen as reinforcing the notion of an embryonic campus development, providing a pair of belated gatehouses to frame the visitor's view of the major Schlumberger pavilion, **9**.

The new building's constituent blocks are conjoined about a central double-height atrium which contains the vertical circulation for the two new accommodation floors and contains the reception desk. An early scheme for the new building incorporated a top-lit lamella-structure tunnel which would have delivered the visitor up onto the winter garden floor, **10**. At a late stage in the design, however, the architects decided that this was far too elaborate a gesture and the route between old and new is now a simple broad walk located on the principal north–south axis which runs from the car park, through the reception point, to the winter garden and test station. The open courtyard between the two structures is planted formally with beech hedges and lavender beds in continuation of the original landscape theme.

Process and precedent
The new building provides Schlumberger with additional scientists' rooms, laboratories, computer and conference rooms along with relocated reception and administrative departments. Although it clearly falls back on the atrium-

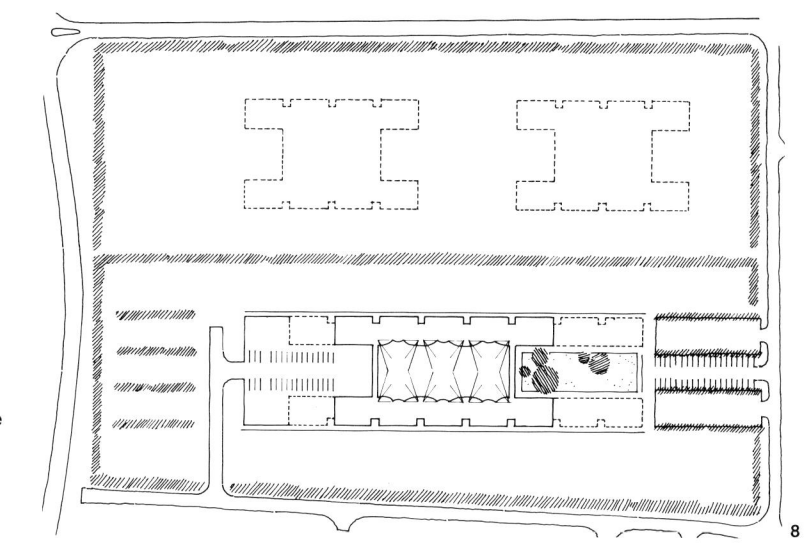

8 Hopkins' early proposals for Schlumberger's expansion on the site anticipated the linear growth of the test station building with the future possibility of adding satellite pavilions alongside it.

9 The reception building appears as a pair of gatehouses in front of the original pavilion.

10 An early scheme for the reception building incorporated a lamella structure tunnel linking it with the winter garden.

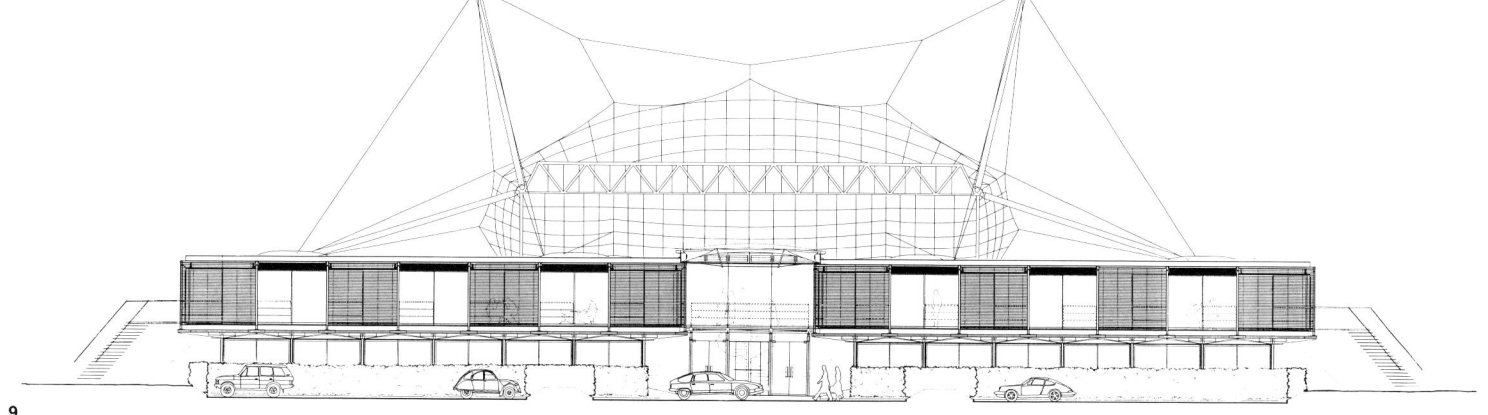

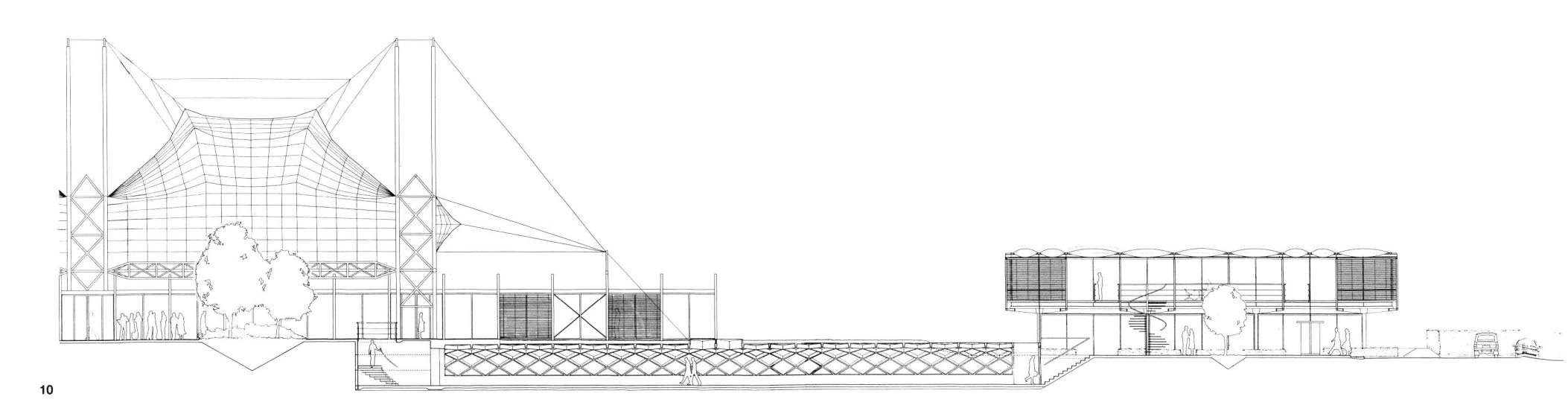

based *parti* of Hopkins' headquarters building for Solid State Logic at Oxford, 1988, **11**, characteristically, it makes many technical advances, most notably in the design of the pneumatic roof above the atrium and the ferro-cement first-floor slabs.

Hopkins' formulation of these two elements demonstrates that the range of his dexterity in manipulating novel technologies is as great as his skill in advancing the capabilities of existing techniques.

At the light end of this spectrum, the air-filled roof cushions, **12**, are constructed from three layers of PTFE sheet, a transparent fluorocarbon film which allows a far higher degree of light penetration than the woven fabric used to roof the winter garden and test station. A silver dot-matrix coating applied to the underside of the top sheet inhibits the effect of solar gain without reducing this transparency significantly. The envelopes are filled with dehumidified air to reduce the risk of condensation forming inside them and can be inflated and pressure balanced by means of air-feed pipes incorporated in the rectangular steel framing structure into which they locate.

The coffered first-floor slab, although it takes forward many of the ideas present in the Solid State Logic building in the way in which it integrates services and structure, is far more expressive than anything seen before in Hopkins' work. Its startlingly sculptural ceiling, **13**, **14**, is strongly reminiscent of Pier Luigi Nervi's Gatti wool factory, Rome, 1951, where the soffit profile portrays literally the isostatic lines of force within the floor slab. Ferro-cement is an obligingly adaptable and durable medium as Renzo Piano and the structural engineer Peter Rice demonstrated in the design of the light reflecting roof louvres for the Menil Gallery, Houston, 1987.

At Schlumberger, the complex slab geometry was generated in part, by a requirement to place the ground-floor internal columns on the half-beat of the rhythm set by those on the perimeter. On the first floor, the columns are cantilevered out on finger-like projections in the slab, **15**, and follow yet another offset, bringing them onto grid with those in the interior.

Such structural juggling produces a slab profile of genuine complexity and beauty which belies the simplicity of the technique that produced it. The ferro-cement element of the slab is actually only a thin shell, factory made by spraying aerated mortar into a mould containing expanded metal mesh. These shells are brought together on site and supported temporarily while a reinforced concrete slab is cast into them, **16**, **17**. In effect, this method is analogous to the technique of permanent shuttering, the key difference being that the concrete bonds to the ferro-cement as it cures so that the two elements form a single structure.

11 Hopkins' headquarters building for Solid State Logic, Oxford, 1988.
12 The roof above the atrium in the reception building relies on a series of air-filled cushions constructed from three layers of PTFE sheet.
13, 14 The reception building's coffered first-floor slab integrates services and structure in a remarkably sculptural way.
15 Detail of the finger-like projections at the slab edge which support the first-floor columns.

Shifting ground

Aside from the shifting structural preoccupations that Schlumberger's new building may be seen to highlight in Hopkins' work, it also represents a shift in the development of the company's research techniques towards a greater emphasis on theoretical and computer modelled studies and away from practical experiment. In formal terms, this has led to a greater reliance on highly serviced and environmentally-controlled spaces radically different in conception to the test station which still remains in use, **18**.

Each of the two-storey blocks in the new building comprises two square concentric rings of scientists' rooms which wrap a laboratory and computer room in one instance, and a laboratory and conference suite in the other. The scientists' rooms are set out on the original building's 3.6m planning module, thus maintaining the space standards that Schlumberger considers appropriate while forming an element of visual unity between the two structures in the rhythm and detail of their external envelopes: the full-height glazing and electrically-operated blinds which feature strongly in the new building have been copied from the earlier office wings, **19**.

Like its formative predecessor, the Solid State Logic building, the first-floor slabs of the new Schlumberger building cantilever out to shade the ground floor. This gesture also has the merit of reducing the building's apparent bulk. The roofline has been kept deliberately low to achieve a balanced relationship with the test station building. This has been achieved partly by keeping floor-to-ceiling heights to a minimum and partly by setting the new ground floor level 600mm below the datum of the winter garden, a move that was made possible by the site's falling contours.

Site and servicing

Schlumberger's site at High Cross occupies relatively high ground, allowing its inhabitants the advantage of long views south across working farmland and east to the college spires which offer a distant echo of the building's booms and cables on the flat Cambridgeshire skyline, **20**. The site section has always been used to strong advantage.

In the test station building, the office and laboratory blocks are arranged north–south on the plot in two single-storey strips. Between them is a 24m wide zone occupied by the test station and winter garden. The winter garden is placed on the crest of the site, establishing the centre's principal floor level. Taking a datum from the services entry point at the northern end of the building, a lower level, 2.5m below the winter garden floor, is cut into the rising ground to accommodate the 10m clear height required for the 10 tonne gantry crane that tracks above the test station, and to create a services undercroft which reaches out beneath the two wing blocks, **21**.

16, 17 Views of the first-floor slab under construction. The ferro cement shells are supported while a reinforced concrete slab is cast into them. **18** Schlumberger's test station gives the centre its practical experimental focus. **19** The reception building's perimeter blinds and glazing are detailed to match the earlier building's laboratory wings. **20** An early Hopkins sketch in which Schlumberger's masted profile echoes the Cambridge spires and **21** showing how the site's rising profile allowed the insertion of a services undercroft beneath the test station.

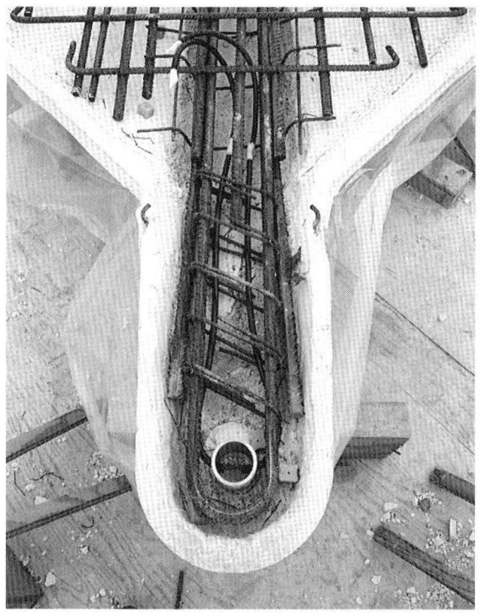

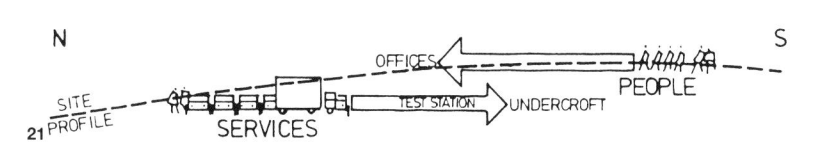

Here Hopkins follows a precedent set by Piano and Rogers in their building for PA Technology, Cambridge, 1975, **22**. Designed for a research-based company, whose organizational requirements are similar to Schlumberger's, it has a highly accessible and easily maintainable basement services distribution network that can be up-dated at will to suit changes in the building's programme.

In the original Schlumberger building, all wet and dry services are directed through the undercroft and up into the laboratories, offices and ancillary rooms. In the laboratories, air-conditioning supply and extract, power, gas, water and drainage all enter from below and are then routed through ducts and outlets in the demountable internal partitions and purpose-made fitted furniture. Toxic gases and foul air from fume cupboards are vented downwards into PVC ducts in the undercroft and drawn out to an exhaust air chimney at the northern end of the building. A raised aluminium grillage floor in the test station, like that of a ship's engine room, allows ductwork to cross over between the wings, and enables service runs to reach all the various experimental installations.

The scale of environmental control that Hopkins applies to individual spaces in the test station building reinforces the centre's spatial spectrum. There is full air-conditioning for the laboratories; basic heating, sun-shading and opening windows for the scientists' rooms; unheated volume for the test station, appropriate to the industrial environment of oil test rigs; and a conservatory atmosphere for the south-facing winter garden which forms a transitional environment between the scientists and the outside world, **23**.

The test station and winter garden can be considered as simple shelters rather than conventional built enclosures. The fabric membrane has little insulative value and the spaces are only partially heated in cold weather, by high-level fan convectors and by passive heat loss from the adjacent laboratories. In the summer however, the fabric membrane provides a high degree of natural sun-shading, keeping the internal temperature close to the required ambient level. When necessary, cooling can be controlled by opening high-level vents in the prismatic roof truss glazing with which Hopkins articulates the three fabric covered bays.

Test station technology

The vital statistics of a drilling test rig in action are mind-boggling. Operating in any one of three vertical shafts ranging from 6 to 20m deep, a full-size commercial bit cuts into rock samples of up to 6m diameter which can be held under near-real levels of temperature and pressure found at depths of up to 5km below the earth's surface. A maximum of 45 tonnes of additional weight can be imposed on the bit while it operates at rotary speeds covering the full commercial drilling range.

22 Piano and Roger's building for PA Technology, Cambridge, a model for Schlumberger's services undercroft.
23 Schlumberger's winter garden and restaurant.
24 The test station's end wall is designed to blow out under blast pressure in the event of an accidental explosion.
25 A laboratory in the test station building.

And almost any natural ground condition can be simulated by bringing in to play a variable flow loop through which mud, oil, gas and water can be pumped to order. For example, liquified mud, fed by two huge 1000 horse power pumps located beneath the machine hall, can be circulated through the rig at a rate of up to 3500 litres per minute before returning to an underground pressure vessel to be cooled and cleaned of rock cuttings prior to recycling.

The test station equipment is designed to induce pressures of up to 10,000 psi at 170°C within elements of the wellbore simulator. It comes as no surprise to find that the explosion risk is taken seriously. The system is designed to release only a limited amount of pressurized material in the event of a mechanical failure; and the resulting blast would primarily be contained within the station's reinforced concrete underground pressure chambers, although the test-station end wall, **24**, is designed to blow out under severe blast pressure.

Confidence in the system is such that Schlumberger's health and safety consultants predict that the glazed walls of the surrounding laboratories would be subject to approximately the same air pressure shock, during such an explosion, as the windows on the perimeter would suffer under severe wind loadings. Nevertheless, safety regulations in the centre forbid access to the test station floor while the system is pressurized. The laboratory window wall allows the best possible visual contact between scientists and the technical operations on the test station floor but quite clearly it has to be both resistant to blast damage and highly sound insulative. Consequently, the windows here are sealed units, glazed with 21mm thick laminated glass, but are otherwise detailed identically to their opening double-glazed counterparts in the perimeter offices.

Given the explosion risk and sound transmission problems involved, one might well have expected the test station to be located away from the laboratories, **25**. In fact early schemes assumed such an arrangement but, as has been discussed, the technical drawbacks were finally seen to be greatly outweighed by the social and organizational advantages of bringing them together. For Hopkins, this solution also had obvious formal and structural attractions, allowing him to overlap the building's large and small scale enclosures in a single coherent composition.

Complementary structures

The structural system that supports Schlumberger's taut membrane roof operates completely independently of the enclosing accommodation blocks. The two systems are overlaid on each other in a highly readable way; one expressively addresses the large spans and major volumes of the test station and winter garden, while the other discretely handles the comparatively small scale of the laboratory and scientists' wings.

The wing blocks rely on a customized version of the Patera system which Hopkins developed and patented in 1981 in response to a perceived demand for high quality 'off the peg' light industrial structures, **26**. Patera was intended to be a kind of new generation *Portakabin*, a reinvestigation of Buckminster Fuller's Dymaxion dream of a mass-produced and globalized enclosure, capable of a variety of uses from nursery units for start-up industries to offices or warehouses. It offered a tubular steel-framed and panel-clad package which could generate flexible enclosures in a range of sizes and configurations. However, the system never went into full production – Hopkins' own office in Marylebone occupies one of the few completed prototypes, a 4300 ft^2 double-height open-plan unit with a free-standing mezzanine block.

Like Patera, the Schlumberger wing block structures, **27**, comprise a ready to assemble kit of parts, supplied in completely prefabricated packages capable of quick erection by a very small site team.

Patera was conceived with an exoskeletal steel structure, not visible from the inside of the building. The modified system at Schlumberger follows this pattern but, like the Hopkins office building, substitutes circular hollow section steel posts, set out here on a 3.6 x 14m grid, for Patera's original trussed columns. These posts have welded lugs to take pin-jointed connections to the floor I-beams, **28**, and the trussed roof beams.

To give the blocks overall lateral stability, they are cross-braced at every sixth bay in the wall plane and rely on full moment connections to the steel purlins in the roof plane. This detail enables Hopkins to avoid visible bracing at roof level, thus heightening the system's perceived elegance and clarity.

Another departure from Patera in its pure form, which incorporates specially developed prefabricated insulated roof panels, is the use of built-up roofing for the wing blocks. The Schlumberger roofs incorporate two levels of thermal insulation: glass fibre insulation panels are suspended below the profiled metal roof decking, while above deck there is foamed polystyrene board tapered to falls and topped with a polymeric waterproof membrane.

This gives a very thermally-efficient roof, with a low U-value, offsetting heat losses through the less efficient full-height perimeter glazing. For these sliding window units, the German subcontractor had to develop special framing extrusions to carry the weight of the 3m high glass panels. Hopkins avoided using solar tinted glass, preferring instead clear double glazing to maximize views out, and providing external louvre blinds to eliminate solar gain.

At Schlumberger however, these blinds were selected rather late in the day. The original intention was to rig

26 Prototype 'Patera' light industrial units being assembled.
27 Schlumberger's wing blocks rely on a customized version of Hopkins' Patera system.
28 Pin-jointed lugs connect floor and roof beams to the perimeter columns in the test station building.
29 An early proposal for canopy shading to the scientists' rooms was rejected in favour of electrically-operated blinds.
30 Computer modelling was used to assist the design of the test station building's enclosure and supporting structure.

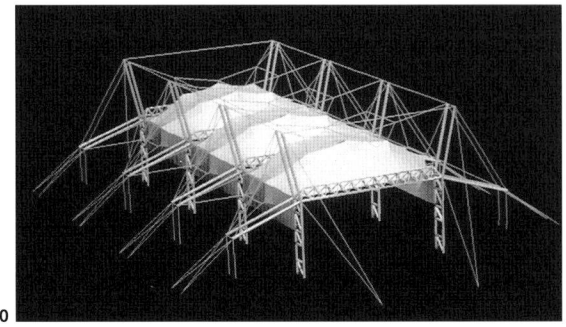

translucent membrane solar shading, cantilevered in a sail profile from tubular steel booms at eaves level, **29**, as Hopkins had done at the Abbey Hill Golf Club in Milton Keynes, 1982. But the blinds as fitted are infinitely more flexible and can be adjusted individually by the scientists. This can lead to a kind of variegated chequerboard pattern emerging along the building during the day as people come and go, but the blinds are automatically reset in the evening, restoring the Miesian clarity of the long office façades.

An expression of tension

The only real continuity between the structure of the test station building's sober wing blocks and the exuberant aerial system that supports the membrane roof is the engineer, Anthony Hunt, who designed both solutions. This might seem an obvious point, but Hunt was not in fact responsible for the design of the roof itself, deferring instead to the lightweight structures division of Ove Arup & Partners. Hunt's task was to provide a free-standing structure for the test station and winter garden enclosures, against which the fabric membrane would be stressed, **30**.

Hunt is a celebrated exponent of the cable-tensioned, pin-jointed structure. Here, the frame is based on a series of tubular lattice towers, linked by prismatic beams, from which raking aerial booms project, connected by 50mm diameter solid steel tension rods. The booms form the support system for the aerial cables which, in turn, connect to node points on the fabric membrane, **31**.

Typically, each four-pinned portal formed by the towers and beams is laterally braced by triangulating tie-rods positioned externally in the entrance wells between perimeter offices in the long wing blocks. Tension from the aerial tie-rods is transferred down from the boom ends into the triangulating ties bracing the portals, **32**. Longitudinal bracing is provided by triangulating tie-rods anchored to intermediate posts in the north and south courtyards, **33**; and by the tubular prismatic trusses that connect all four portals. Similar trusses provide additional lateral bracing at the end portals, in effect forming an articulated ring beam.

Such a complex structure, designed to withstand considerable deflections, demanded a high degree of accuracy in both fabrication and erection; it was consequently detailed to very close tolerances with built-in adjustment points, **34**. The entire test station and winter garden structure is intended to be self-supporting, but it was designed to be 'tuned' as the membranes were erected and it took up the loads, **35**. It incorporates a range of fail-safe mechanisms including the duplication of all critical tensioning members, so that, in the event of a failure, any one tie-rod could support the working load of the building.

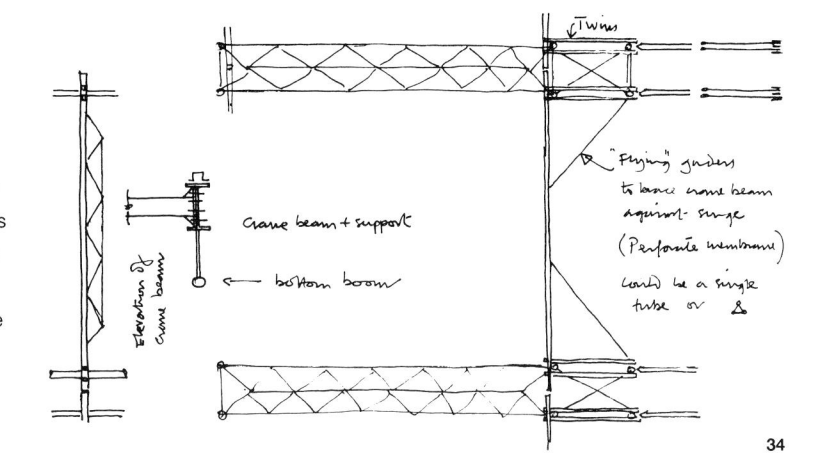

31 Detail of the fabric roof and node-point pick-up assembly.
32 Tension from the aerial tie-rods is transferred from the boom ends down into triangulating ties which are anchored at ground level.
33 Intermediate posts in the north and south courtyards of the test station building provide anchor points for longitudinal bracing.
34 A design sketch by engineer Anthony Hunt exploring Schlumberger's structural system.
35 The test station building under construction, seen during the erection of the membrane roof.

A tented trademark

The fabric membrane roof has become a hallmark of the Hopkins office. Apart from Schlumberger, which was Hopkins' first major venture into fabric technology, there have been unrealized schemes for covering the public concourse at Basildon New Town Centre, 1982–87, **36**; a competition entry for the British Pavilion at the 1992 Seville Exposition, and an initial proposal for a tented version of the Velmead Infants School in Hampshire, 1988. And of course there is the Mound Stand, **37**, at Lord's Cricket Ground, 1987, which represents the current state of the art.[4]

The Mound Stand's membrane roof is made from a PVC-coated woven polyester fibre which differs from the Teflon-coated fabric used two years earlier at Schlumberger. Teflon-coated glass fibre has a class O rating for the surface spread of flame and it does not burn easily. Nevertheless, its use was briefly suspended in the UK because of its tendency to produce toxic fumes in intense fires.

It is well known that the large-scale use of tented structures was pioneered in the 1960s by the German structural engineer Frei Otto. In the mid-1980s, however, Schlumberger represented the first large-scale use of Teflon-coated glass fibre fabric in Britain, beaten to first place only by Terry Farrell's 1982 Clifton Nurseries Building in Covent Garden. Farrell, surprisingly, also gains credit for pioneering the use of PVC-coated polyester fabric in England with a temporary building for Alexandra Palace, completed in 1980.

The use of a fabric enclosure at Schlumberger was never a foregone conclusion. Before committing themselves, Michael Hopkins and John Pringle visited several membrane-covered structures on the west coast of the United States, inspecting Bullocks Department Stores at San Mateo and San Jose and a sports centre with an air-supported roof at Santa Clara. Hopkins came away greatly impressed with the quality of light that the material generated in these buildings and the fact that its durability was proven by more than ten years in use. In fact Teflon-coated glass fibre is considered to be a virtually permanent material with a life expectancy of more than twenty years.

Fabric manufacture

The glass fibre mat used to form the membrane is woven like a conventional cloth with warp (vertical) and weft (transverse) threads. The warp strands are stiffer and straighter than those in the weft, which the weaving process encourages naturally to undulate. Tensioning the fabric involves concentrating the major forces in the direction of the weft, in effect pulling these undulating strands straight.[5]

Allowing for differential stretch is a key factor in calculating the fabric size. The material used at Schlumberger

36 Hopkins' first experiment with fabric technology was a scheme for roofing over the concourse of Basildon New Town Centre, 1982–87.
37 The marquee-like upper deck of Hopkins' Mound Stand, Lord's Cricket Ground, 1987.

typically stretched about 3.2% in the weft and only 0.6% in the warp which meant that it arrived on site 'too small' and had to be tensioned during the erection sequence, **38–43**, to get it to fit. This necessitated complex co-ordination procedures to ensure that the fabric mated accurately with the structure. However, it is worth noting that the problems faced are not new: pre-drilled and hydraulically adjustable fixings were first used in the construction of the Eiffel Tower in the late 1880s.

To maintain tension in the membrane once it is in place, it must be stressed evenly along its leading edges. At Schlumberger this is facilitated by a perimeter detail which incorporates an 8mm diameter steel strand cable in the lapped fabric edge. This allows the membrane to be securely clamped to a continuous angle section, with radiused corners, incorporated in the main structural frame, using a luff-groove detail similar to that used for the sails of racing yachts.

The conjunction of the free geometry of the membrane-covered bays with the prismatic and rectilinear structural skeleton is one of the test station building's most obvious technical and formal successes. The detailing, however, is intentionally simple and direct. The 100 x 100mm steel angle welded to the principal tubular members also serves as a gutter along the roof edge, although water run-off from the three membrane-covered bays is ultimately directed onto the flat roofs of the wing blocks. There is no intermediate gutter or drainage channel between the roof fabric and the wings; the rainwater run off from the tented roof is simply directed onto the wing blocks and drained away through concealed downpipes.

Determining the details

The nature of the fabric manufacturing process is such that the width of the material is limited. To cover large spans, or to achieve complex profiles, the fabric is cut to length in strips and then joined to form large sheets using heat-welded seams. This is a factory process which demands great precision in calculating the size of the strips and in pattern cutting and assembly.

Responsibility for calculating the exact profiles of Schlumberger's three 1000m^2 bays fell to the team led by Brian Forster at Ove Arup & Partners. The approximate design was established empirically, using small-scale mock-ups. Then, using a sophisticated computer model, the Arup team was able to set the exact coordinates and consider all the individual and interdependent components of the design, including: the dimensions of the constituent fabric strips; the surface and three-dimensional geometry of the roof; the best pre-tensioning technique; and the likely live and dead loadings from wind, snow and routine maintenance access on the completed structure. This information was then passed to

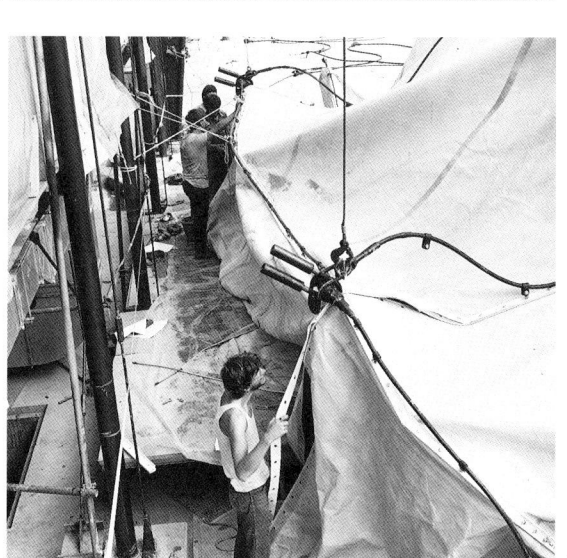

38–43 Construction sequence showing the erection of the test station's fabric roof. The fabric arrived on site 'too small' and was tensioned during the erection process to get it to fit. The fabric is stressed evenly along its leading edges to ensure that tension is maintained once it is in place.

the membrane subcontractor, Stromeyer Ingenieurbau GmbH, who carried the design through to the precise detailing of individual components and junctions, producing large-scale drawings for the architect's and engineer's approval, **44**.

Many individual areas of both the test station and the reception buildings were in fact designed in this way, and not detailed in the Hopkins office as one might have expected. Hopkins prefers to use a form of management contract in which the architect is responsible for the initial detailed design and the contractor takes charge of its implementation. Under this system, the architect sets out a detailed performance specification and a set of visual criteria for each sub-contract package which the subcontractors must meet and the general contractor must underwrite. The business building thus becomes a three way process in which the manufacturer informs the design process.

There are drawbacks of course. The final details of any particular element of the building are never known until the subcontractor has been appointed. And this can lead to delays if, for whatever reason, he is not selected at the appropriate time. But Hopkins finds that this way of working suits the office very well. It means that they can get to know a set of subcontractors, building up a working relationship with them over several projects, just as the traditional architect historically assembled a group of favoured craftsmen.

Hopkins, High-tech and history

The test station and reception buildings of Schlumberger Cambridge Research are perhaps archetypal High-tech structures – free-standing pavilions on a green field site, with a lightweight system of construction, employing new materials. And Hopkins, on the face of it, is perhaps the archetypal High-tech architect: a self-proclaimed pragmatist, technologist and technocrat. However, behind this façade hides a far more complex designer.

Paradoxically, the Schlumberger buildings are very much hand-crafted, despite their machine-made aesthetic. Indeed they evince the value of craft in a predominantly de-skilled building industry. Both are one-offs, working prototypes, conceived and executed with great precision, and built under pressure, without room for mistakes or time to rehearse. Both also have a strong visual identity: one is an expressive structure that addresses a broad range of issues: the provision of a comfortable and egalitarian working environment across a range of spatial options; the creation of a sense of space, and of place, in a building whose structure and services must be inherently flexible; free planning versus formal control; and the elaboration of a form appropriate to a modern technological process and a forward-looking client. The other speaks of consolidation, reinforcing the formal discipline of the earlier building on the site.

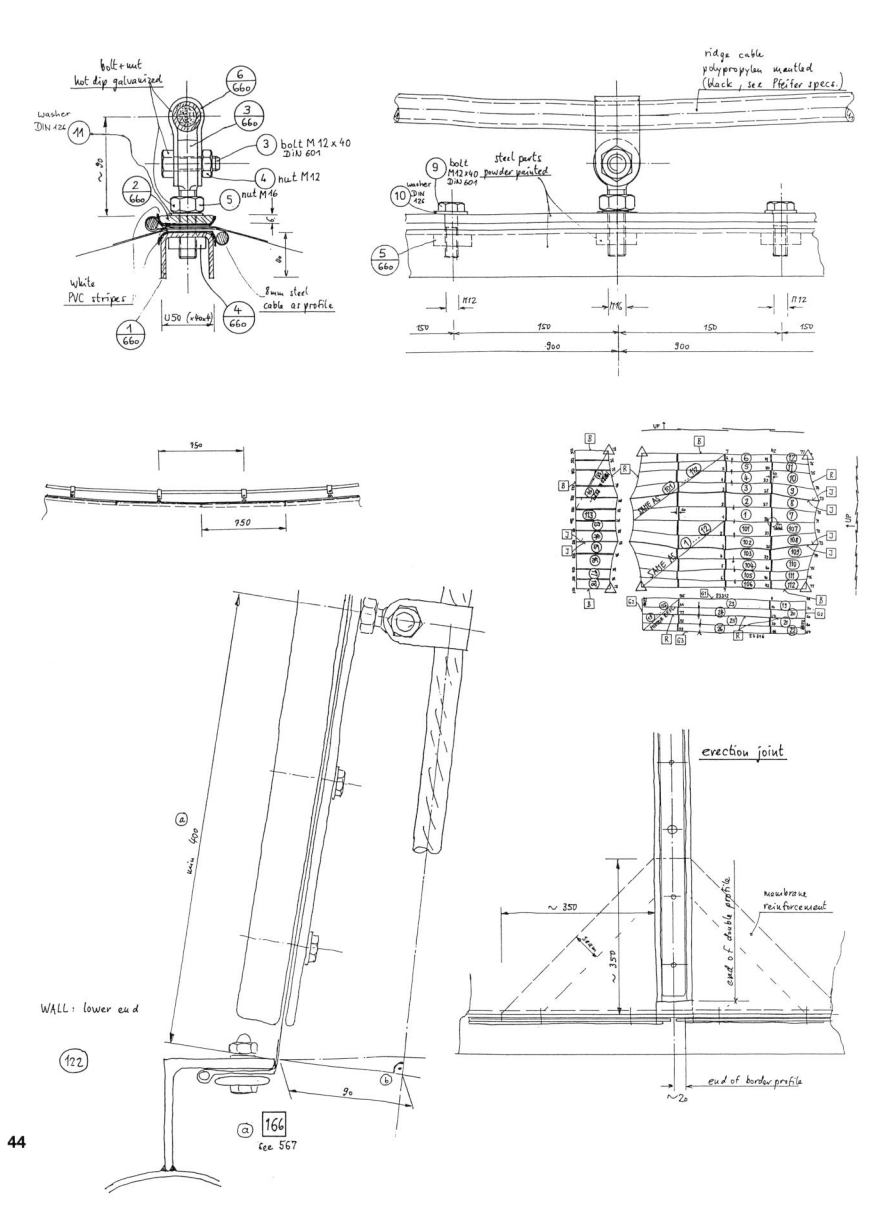

44 Extracts from the working drawings produced by the fabric roof subcontractor for the architect's and engineer's approval.
45 Michael and Patty Hopkins' own house in Hampstead, London.
46 Detail of the brick arcade of Hopkins' Mound Stand, evidence of his readiness to investigate traditional technologies.
47 Mies van der Rohe, Crown Hall, IIT campus, 1952–56.
48 Mies van der Rohe, Farnsworth House, 1946.

Hopkins' relationship with his client is close and obviously fruitful; their dialogue has always been informed by clear ideas, but has led nonetheless, in the case of the test station block, to a highly image-conscious building. But such structural rhetoric can be seen as following inevitably from the choice of membrane roof construction; a decision that was made ostensibly on the grounds of translucency, lightness and economy. However, the question of image is inescapable. Generically, the High-tech school maintains the conceit of following an extreme functionalism, while in truth it can be as expressive as Classicism or Post-Modernism.

Hopkins, ever the quiet puritan, would never allow himself the voluble excesses of, say Rogers' Lloyd's building or the Beaubourg. He is closer, naturally, to Foster insofar as his architecture is recognizably systems-based and the technology is generally discreet. His own house, **45**, at Downshire Hill in London, is a coolly classical glass box that owes much to the catalogue-component ethos of Charles Eames. Unfashionably for a High-tech architect, he is also prepared to dip into the back catalogue. The robust brick arcade at the Mound Stand, **46**, is proof of his willingness to embrace traditional technologies when the situation demands it. Echoing Mies van der Rohe, Hopkins maintains that any material, any construction, is acceptable provided it has structural 'clarity'. The pursuit of clarity is perhaps the key to his admiration for Mies, whose deftness of detail and considered juxtaposition of materials is emulated in much of Hopkins' work.

Hopkins made his first visit to Chicago in the summer of 1989 and saw the Mies buildings at the Illinois Institute of Technology and Lake Shore Drive for the first time. He came away, 'heartened by how good they are'. Looking at the plan of Perlstein Hall, 1945–6, for the IIT campus, for example, it is easy to find formal similarities with the original Schlumberger plan and, of course, integrationalist sympathies with the buildings from Hopkins' time at Foster Associates.

Other resonances abound. Mies' use of exoskeletal roof trusses as a device for reducing the apparent depth of the roof zone at Crown Hall, **47**, finds clear echoes at Schlumberger, whose test station wing blocks have the structural panache of Mies on a grand scale, but the domestic qualities of the Farnsworth House, whose famous steps, **48**, are quoted in passages in every 6th bay along the office façades.

Like Hopkins, Mies also understood the value of craft and had a keen historical perspective. He declared in a lecture to the Illinois Institute in 1950, 'Technology is rooted in the past, it dominates the present and tends into the future. It is a real historical movement, one of the great movements which shape and represent their epoch'.[6] Michael Hopkins' work surely evinces the truth of these remarks.

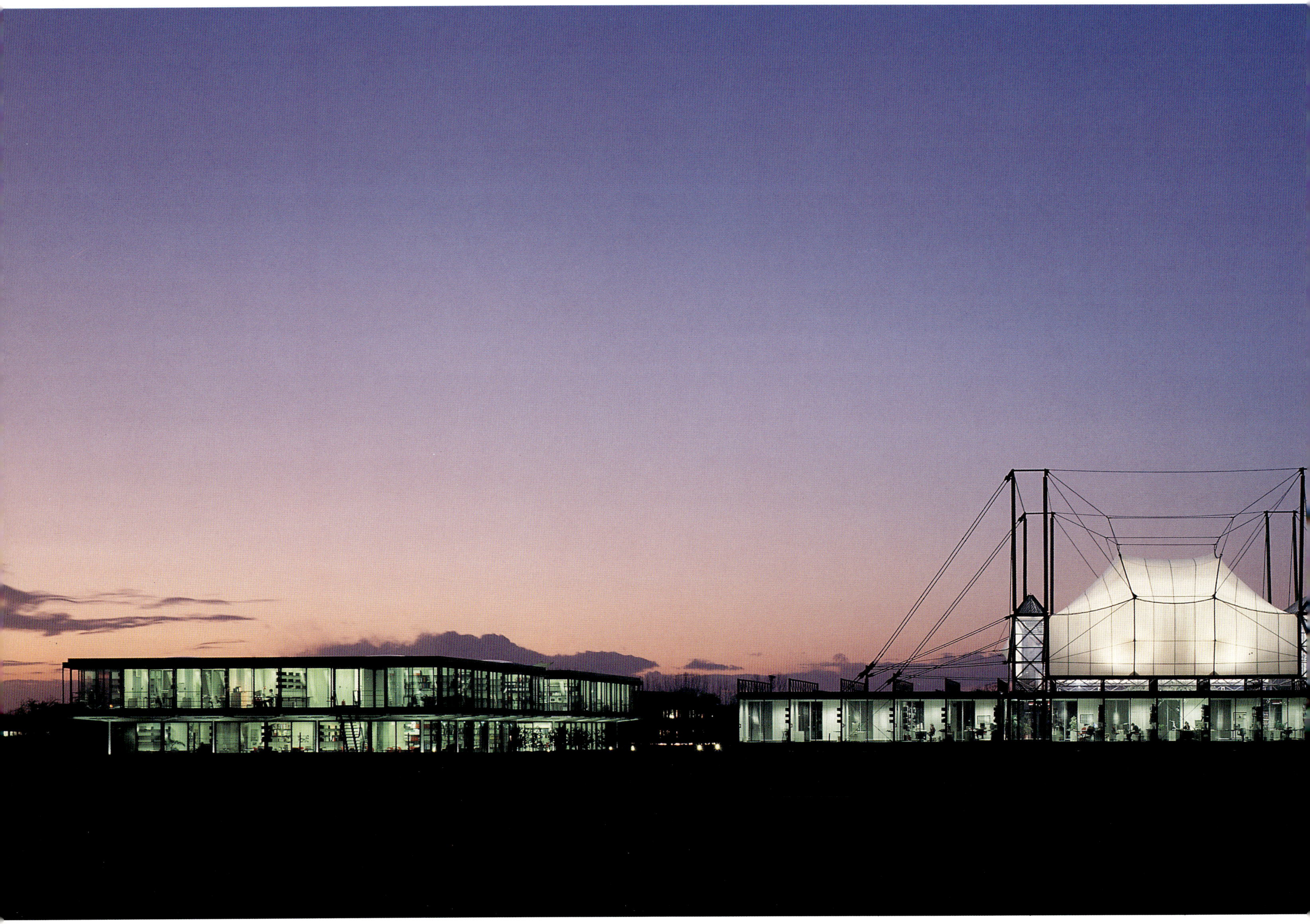

Photographs

Previous spread, Schlumberger at night; its remarkable forms leave a strong impression on the flat Cambridgeshire skyline. Left, a view into the scientists' rooms in the reception building. Right, electrically-operated blinds screen the scientists from glare and sunlight.

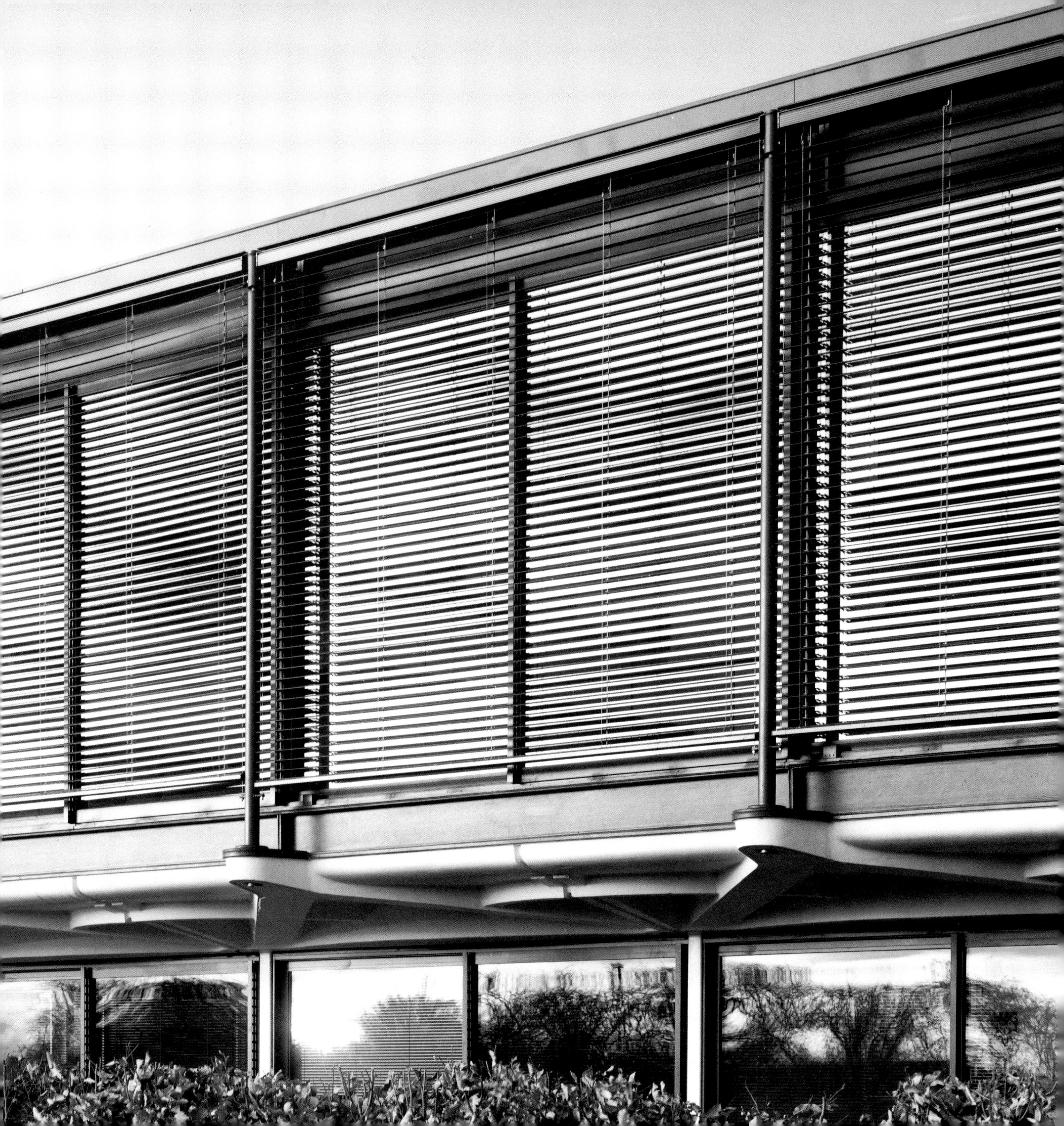

Left, visitors to the Schlumberger centre arrive at the atrium in the reception building. The test station building is reached via a stone covered path across a landscaped courtyard. Right, the view from the bridge; the test station building seen from one of the first-floor crossing points in the reception building. Following pages, details of one of the pair of fabric canopies which shade the glazed end walls of the reception building atrium.

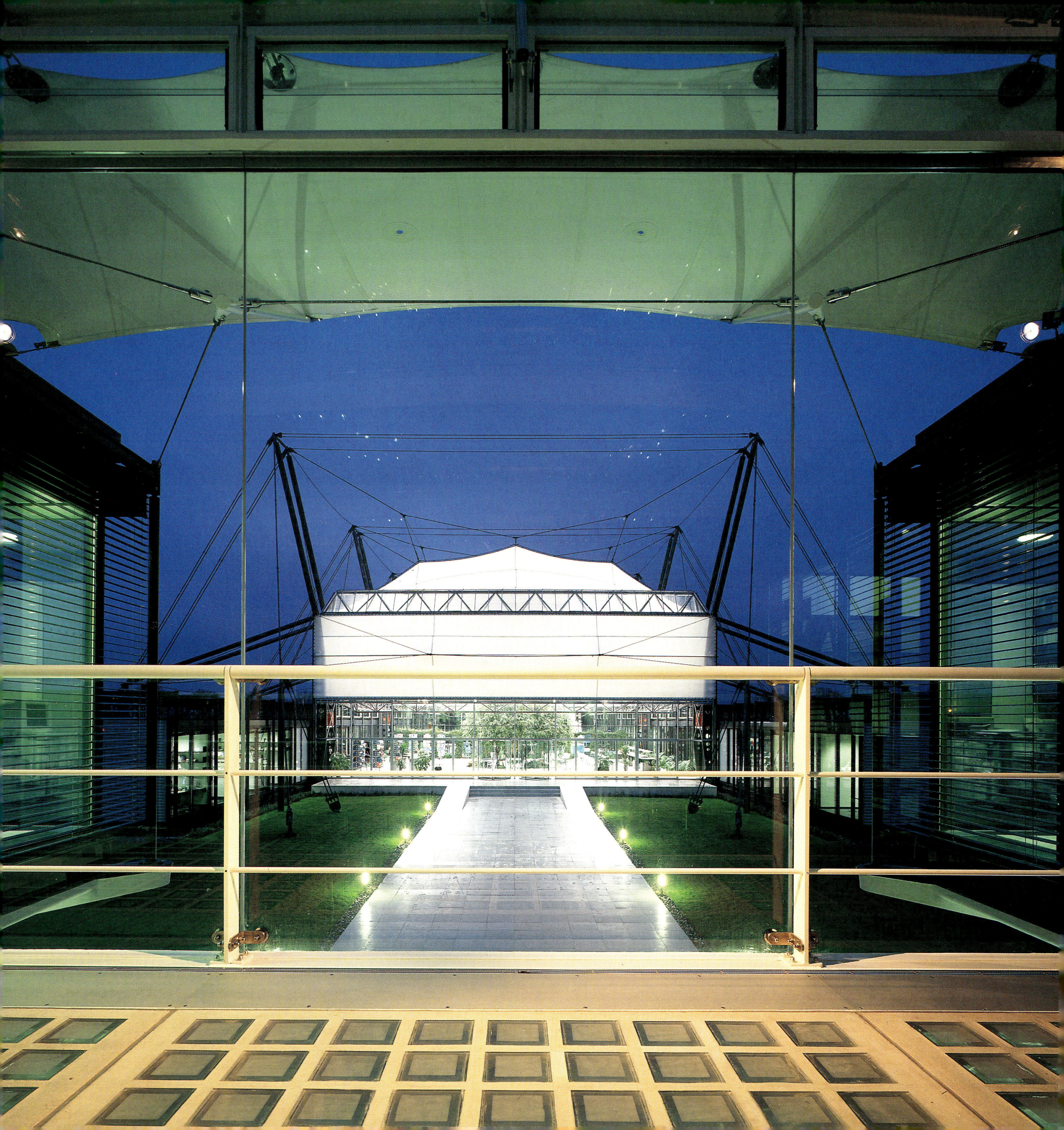

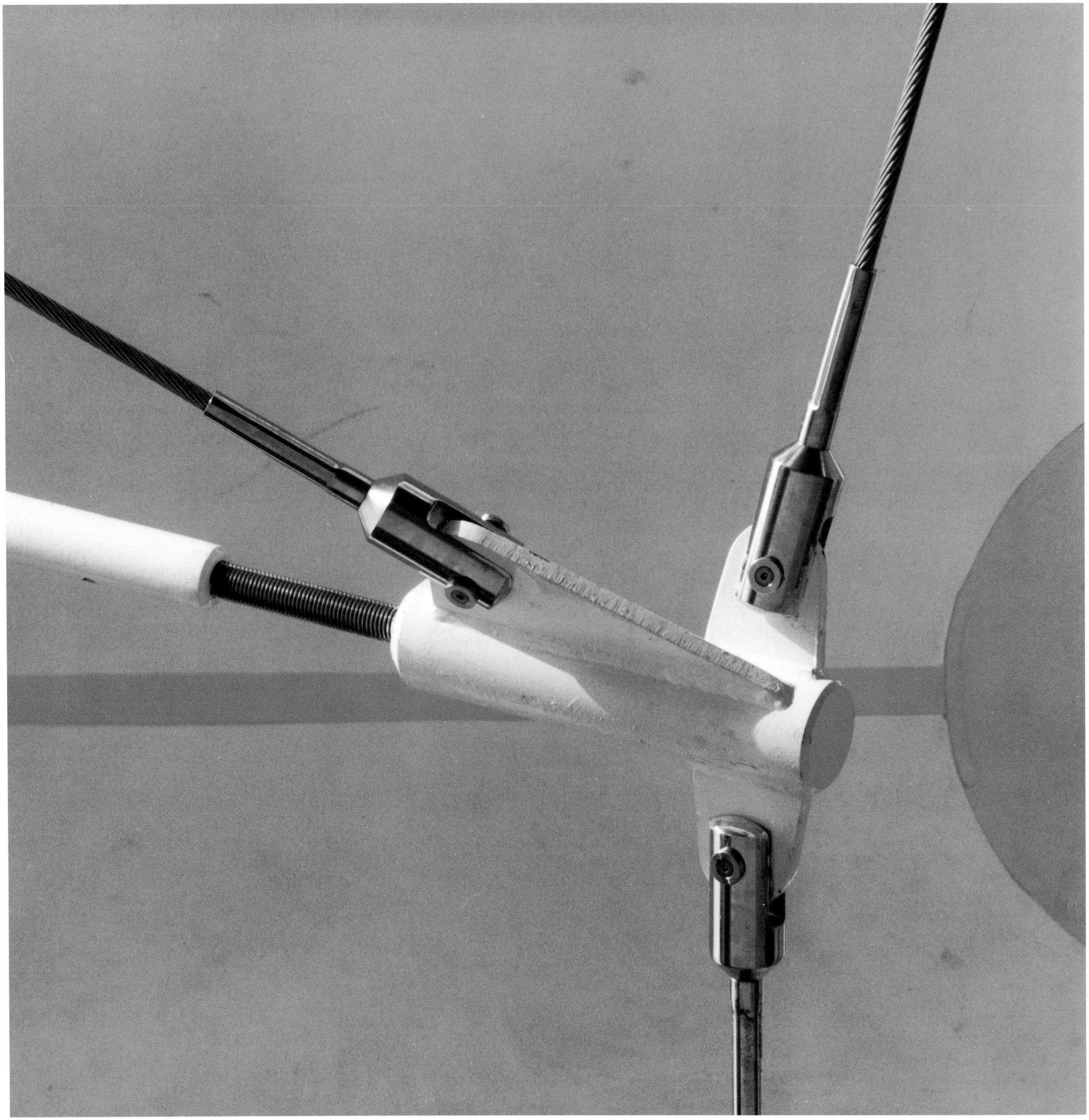

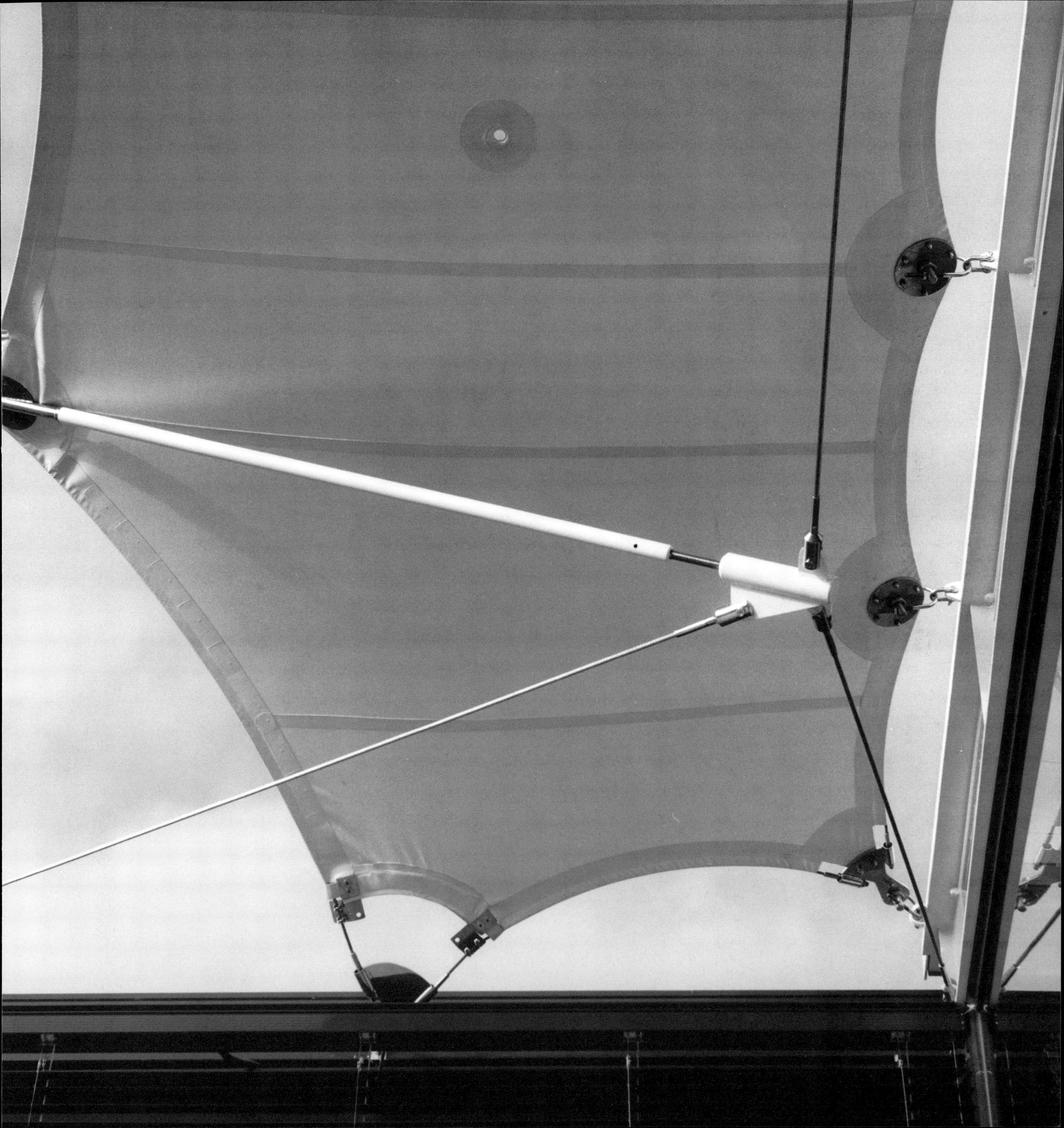

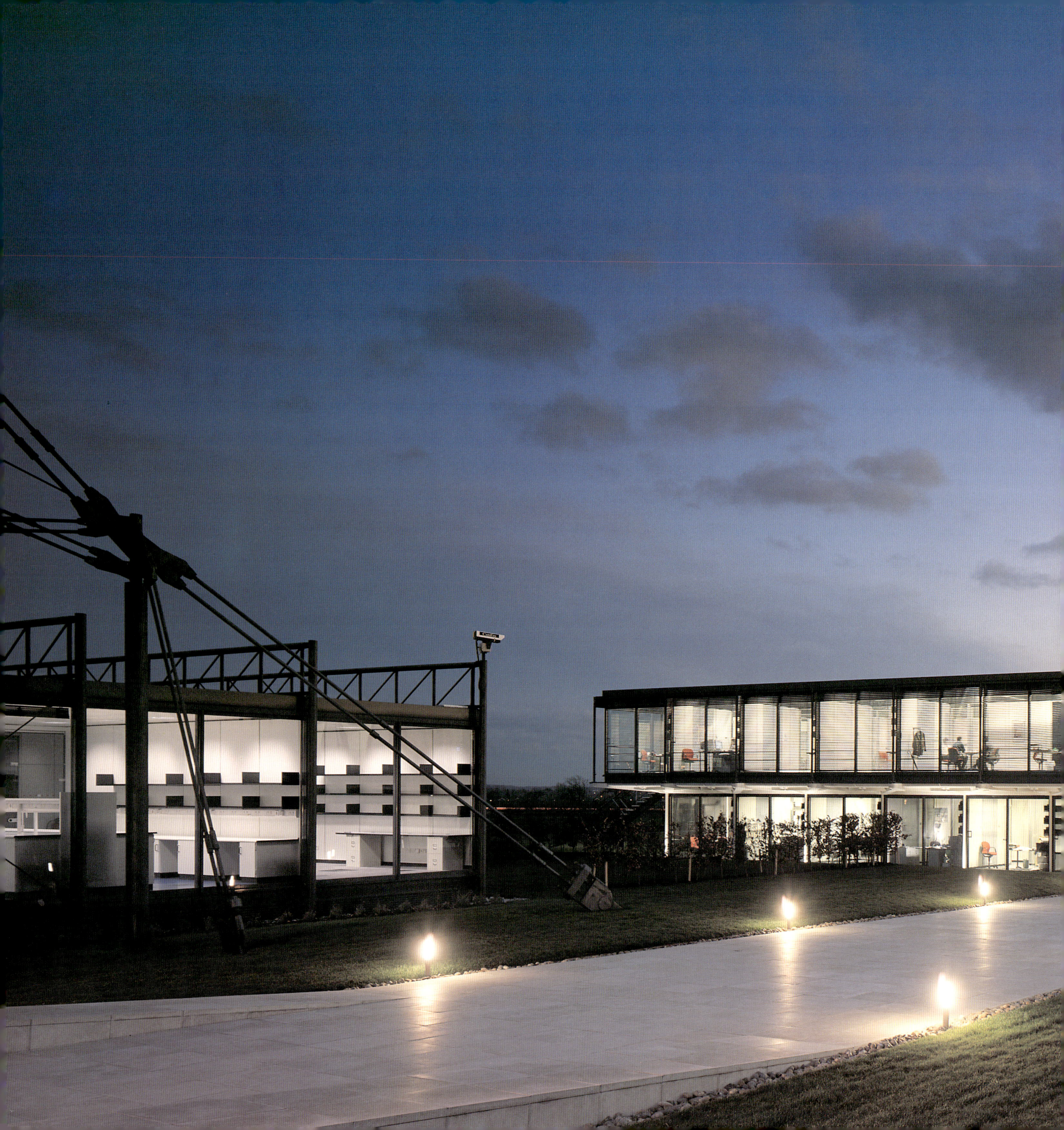

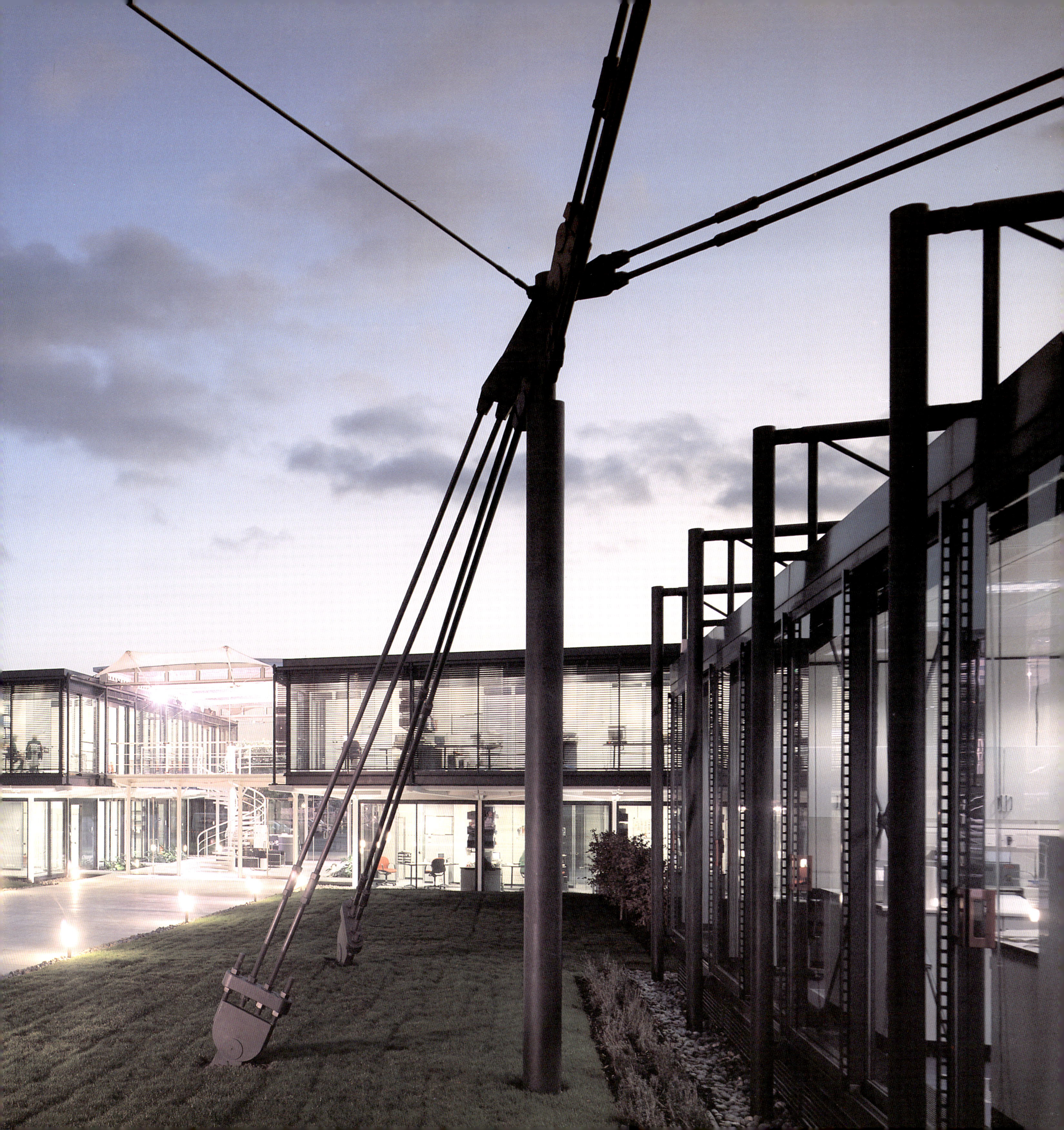

Preceding spread, an early evening view from the terrace outside the test station building towards the reception building. Left, the test station building presents an axially organized, almost *Beaux Arts* front to the approaching visitor. Its formality reinforces the notion of the reception building as a pair of gatehouses before the major Schlumberger pavilion. Right, details of the tensioning cables and fabric which forms the vertical enclosure to the winter garden.

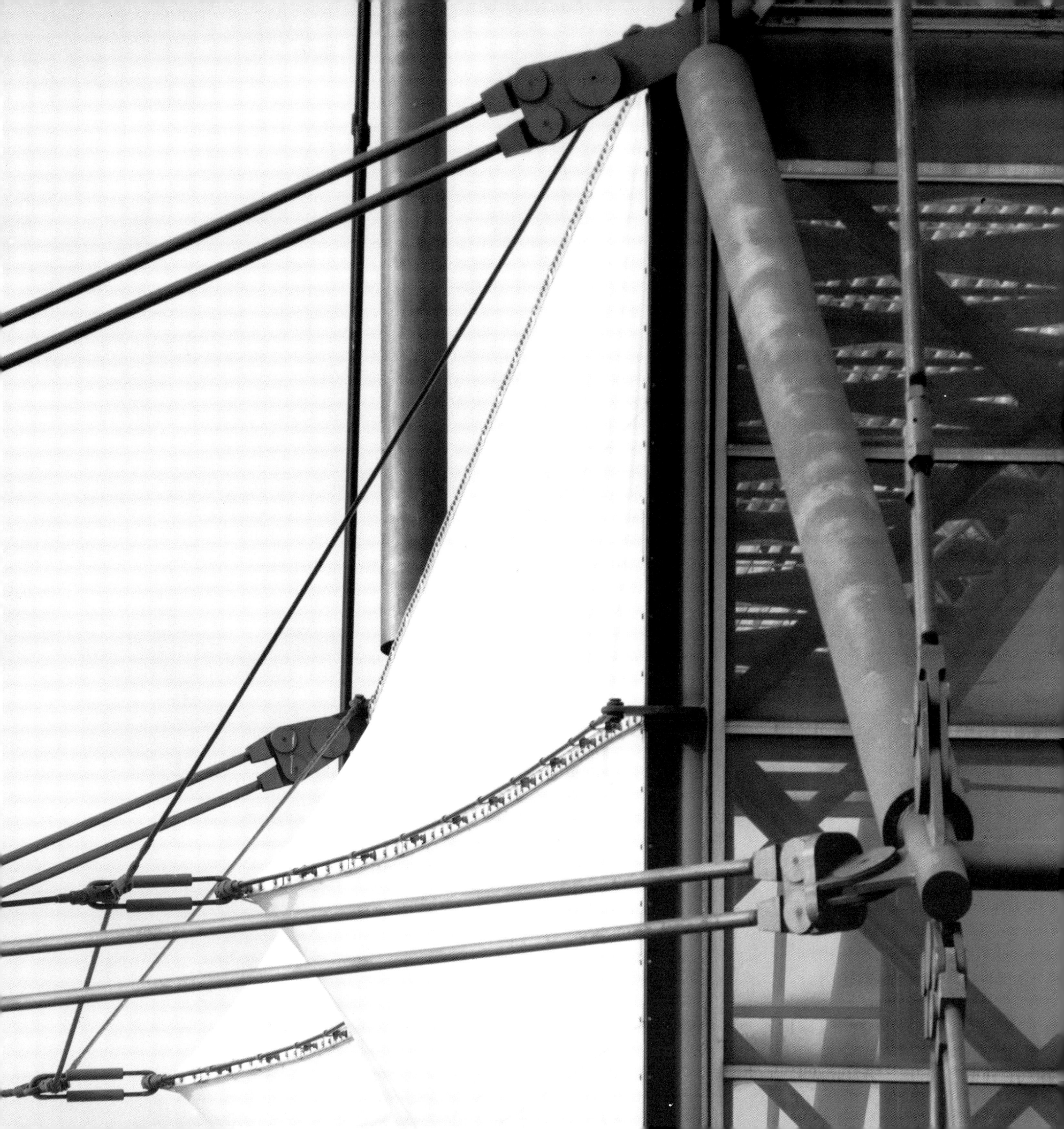

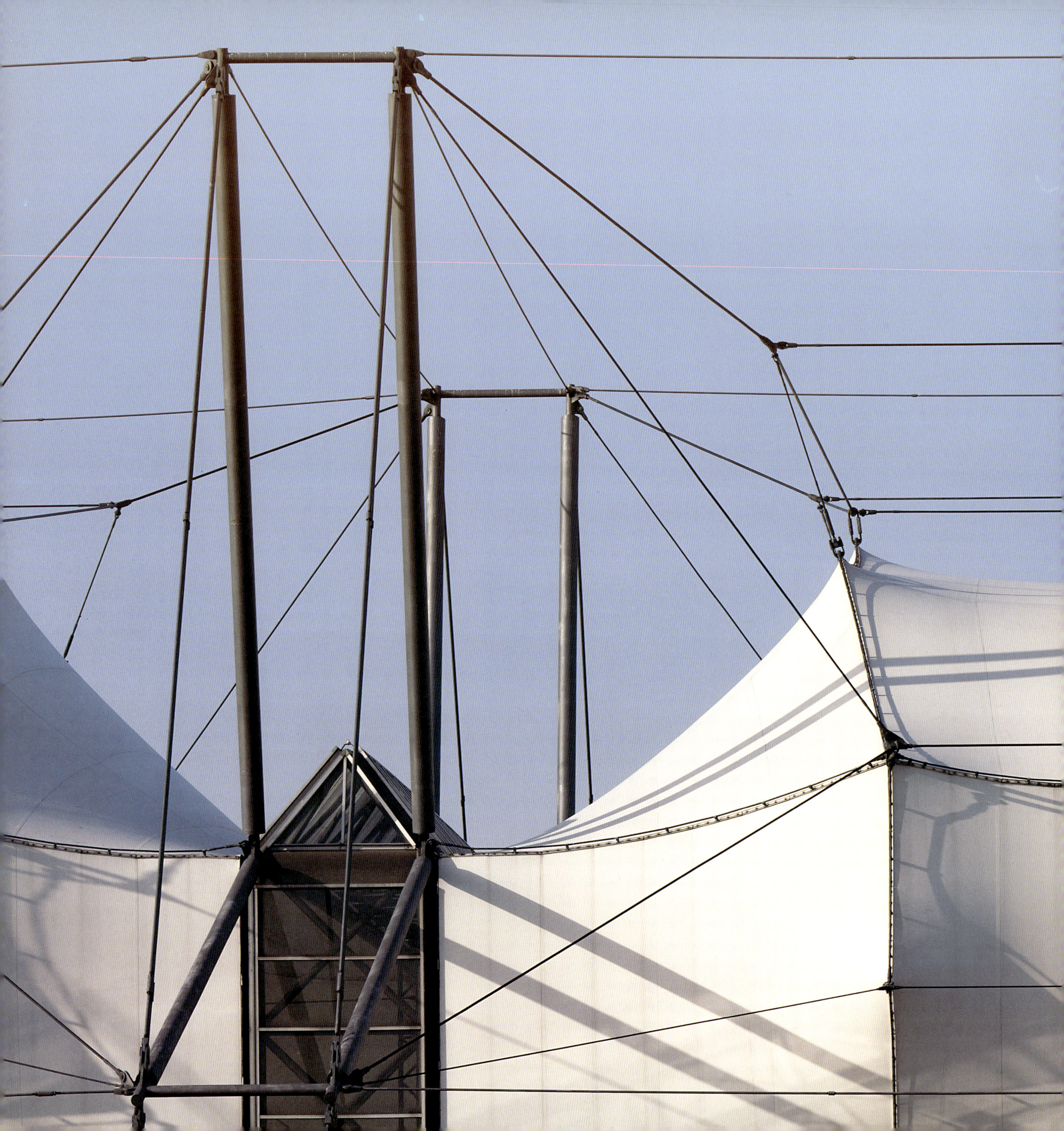

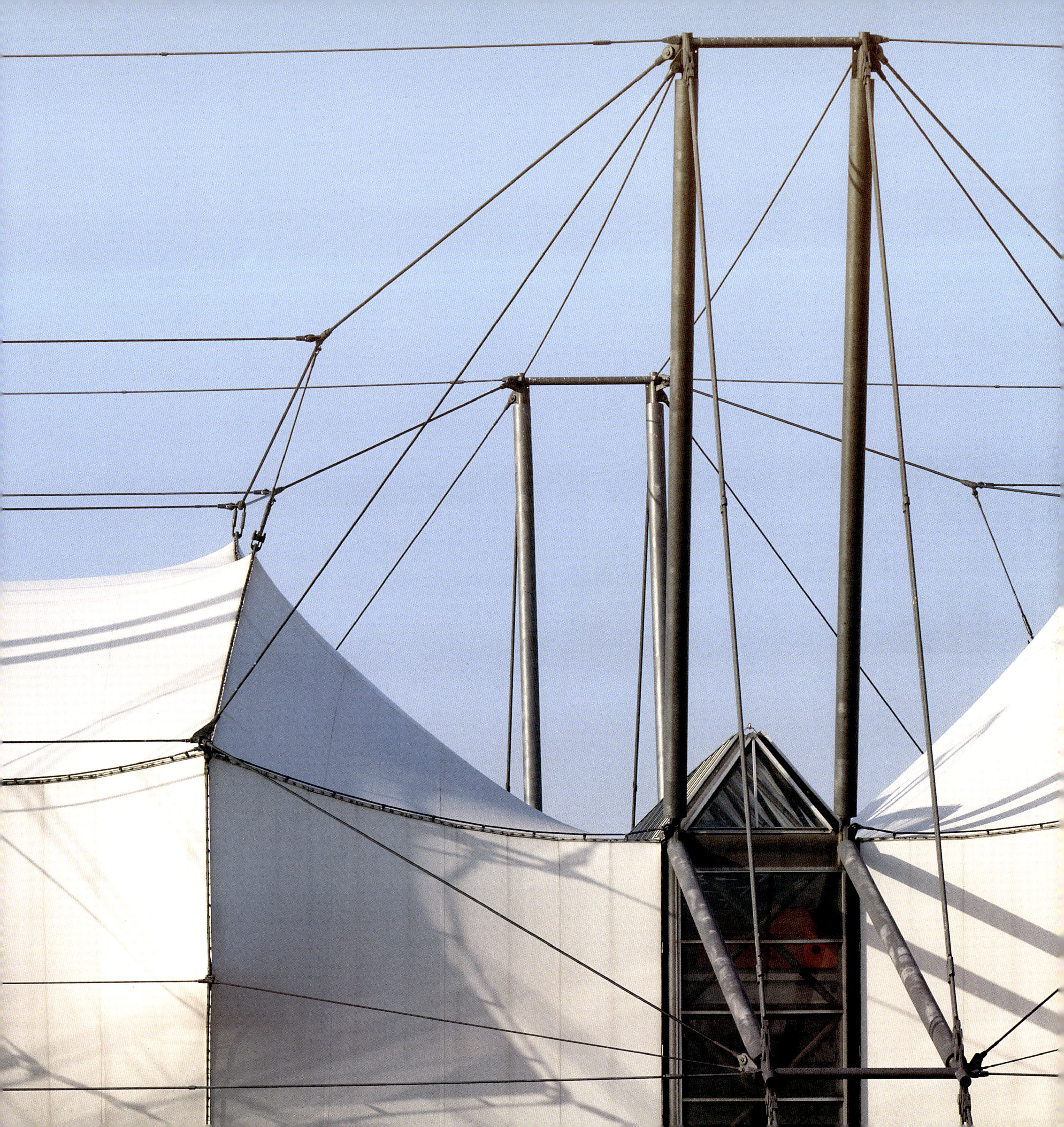

Previous spread and left, detail of one of the fabric-covered bays above the test station. The supporting frame is based on a series of tubular lattice towers, linked by prismatic beams from which aerial booms project; these are connected at their ends by 50mm diameter solid steel tension rods. Each four-pinned portal formed by the towers and beams is braced laterally by triangulating tie rods anchored at ground level in the entrance wells that articulate the long laboratory blocks. Triangulating ties transfer the tension forces down from the aerial tie rods and boom ends to the ground. Right, the booms provide the support system for aerial cables which in turn connect to node points attached to the fabric membrane.

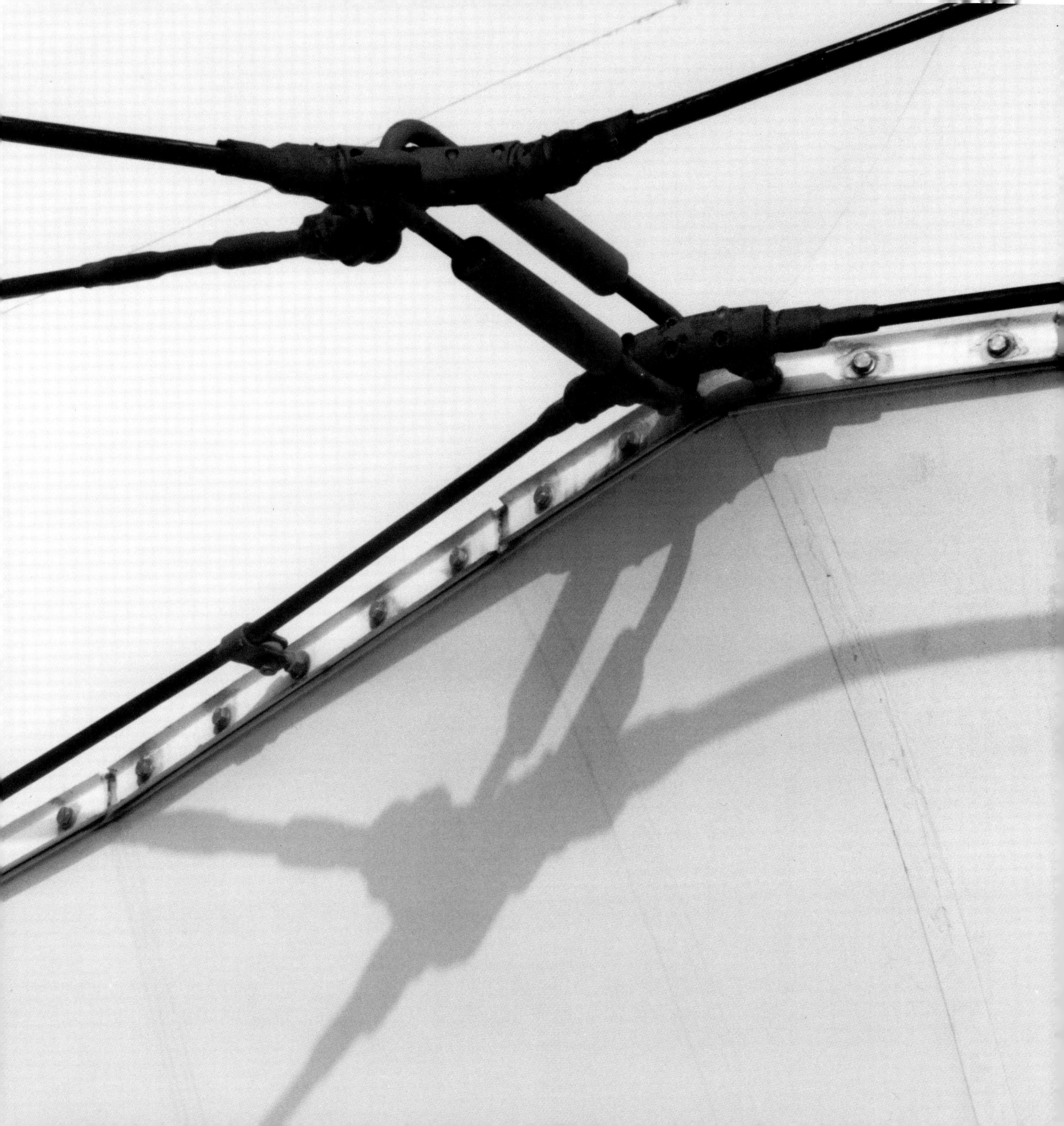

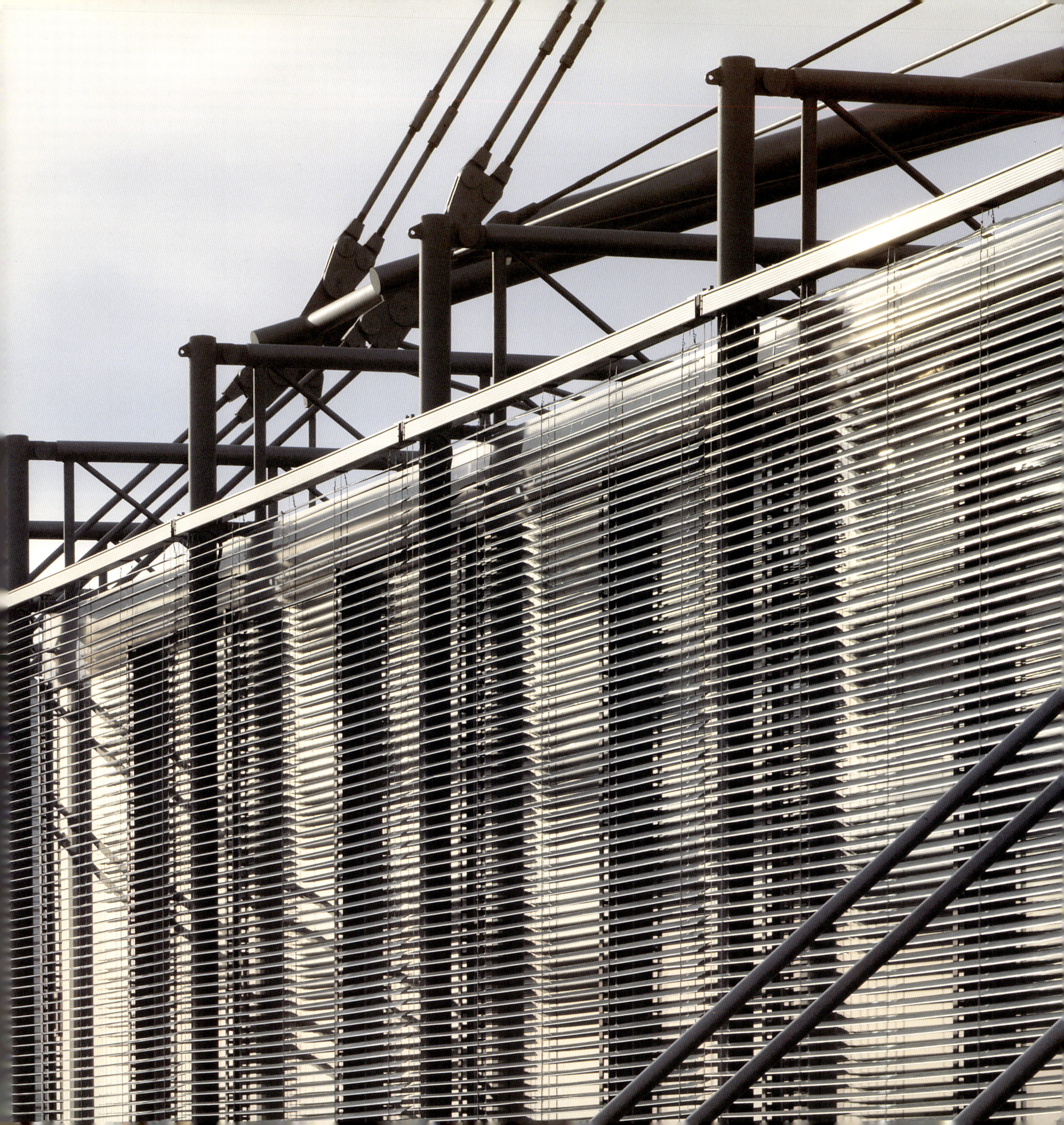

The laboratory wings of the test station building convey an almost Miesian sense of calm and order in sharp contrast to the expressive sculptural force of the fabric roof and rigging.

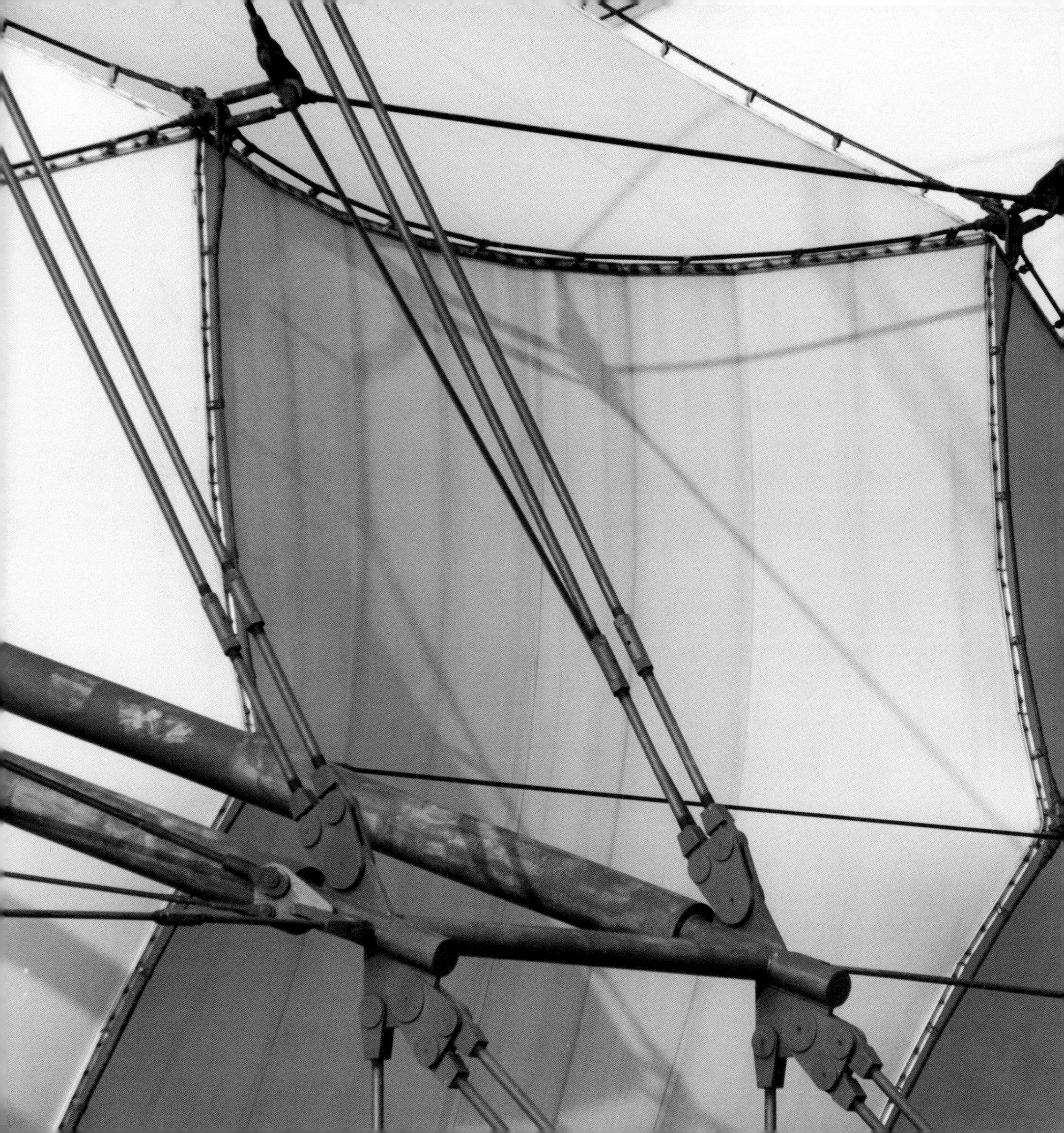

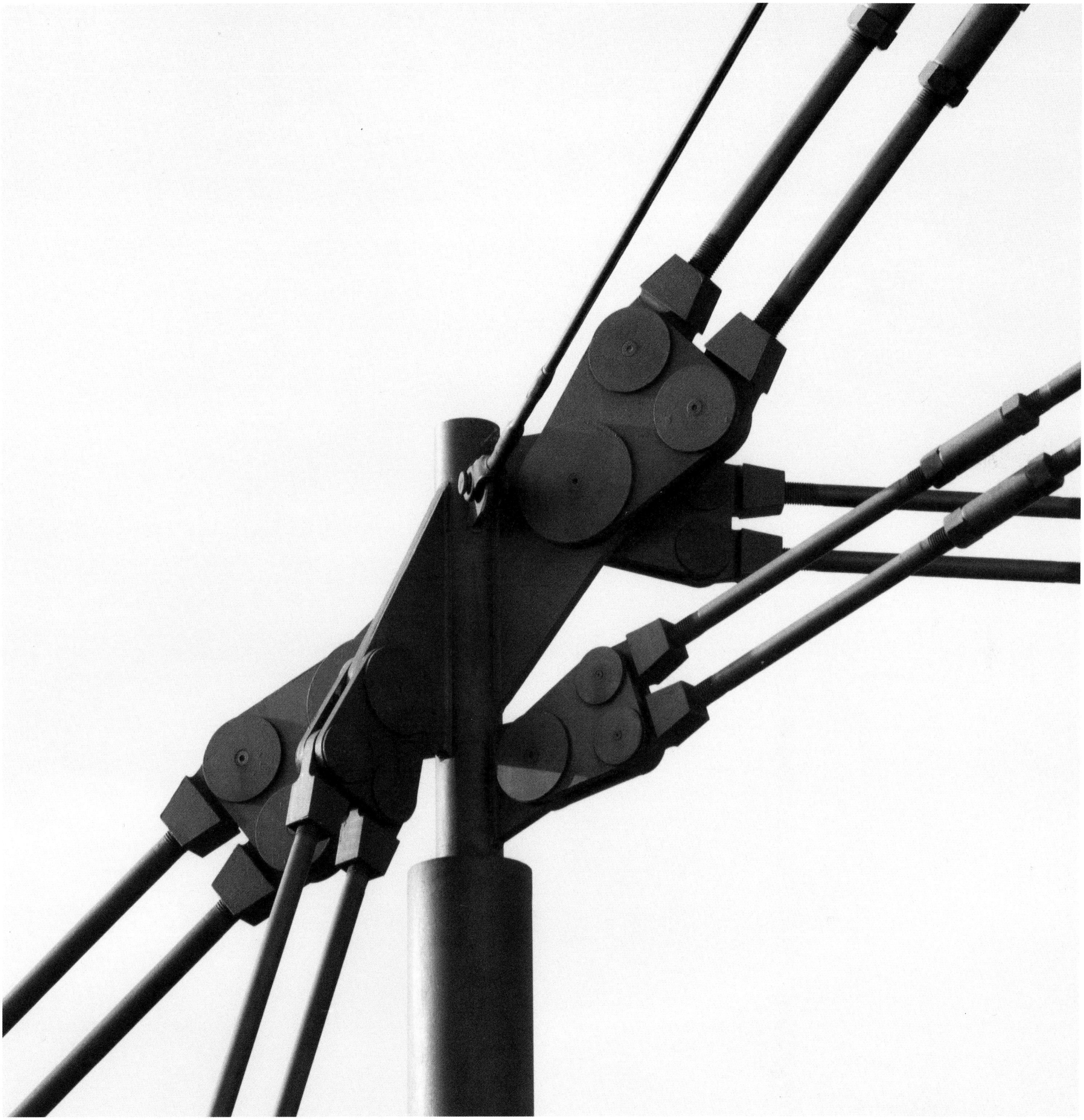

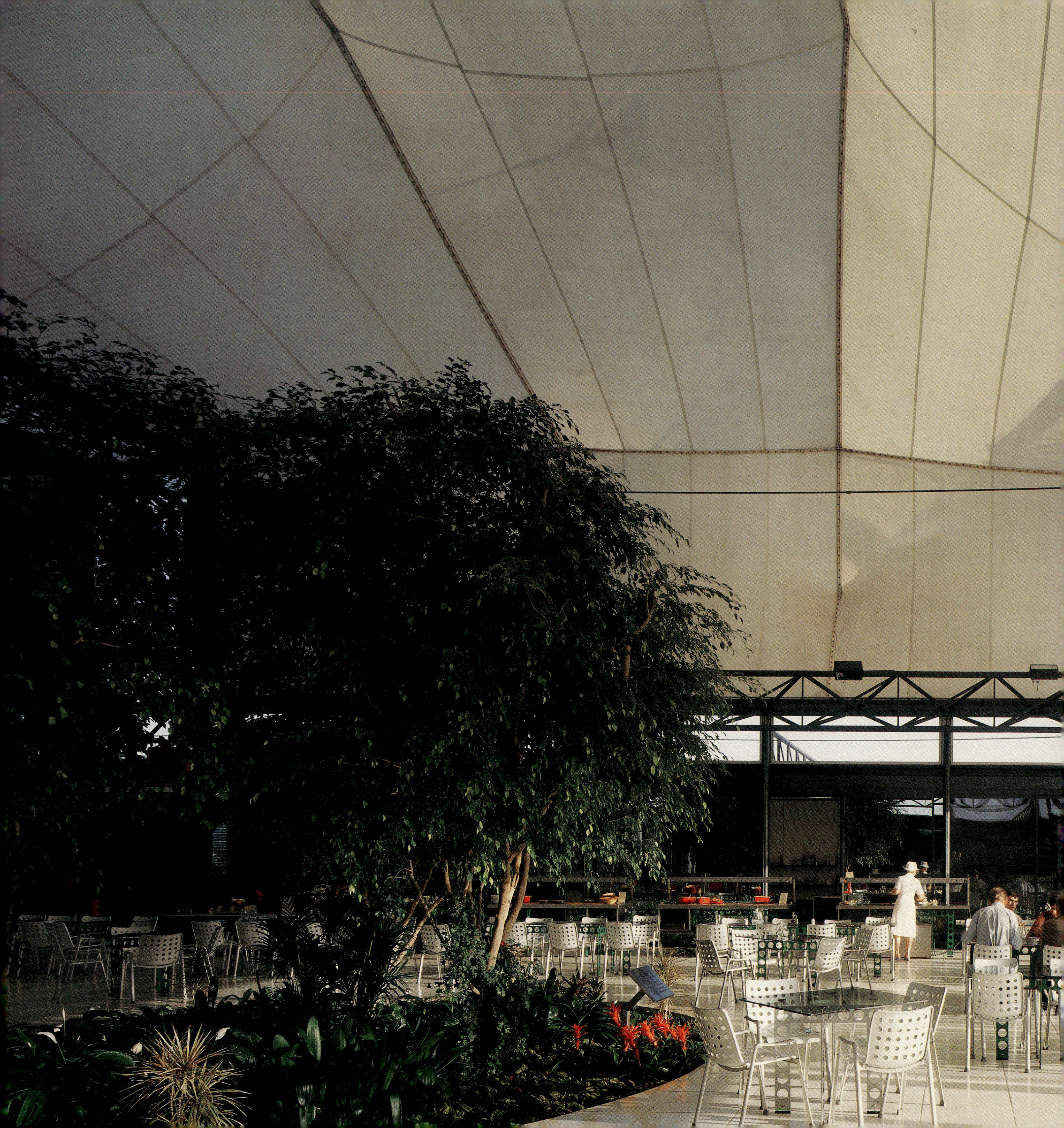

The winter garden provides the Schlumberger centre with a welcoming social focus. Before the completion of the reception building, this space also served as the centre's main foyer in addition to its role as restaurant and meeting point.

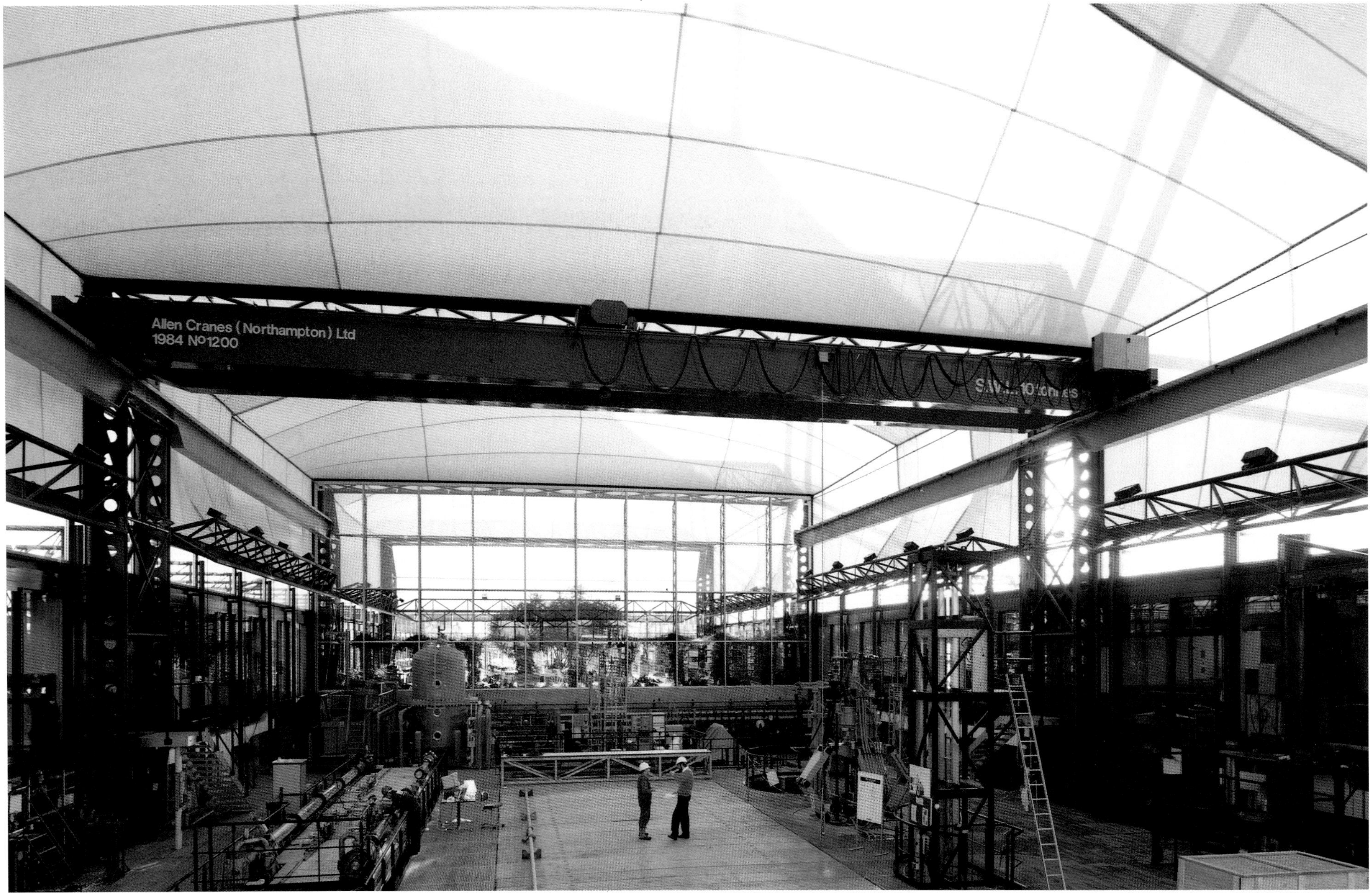
Allen Cranes (Northampton) Ltd
1984 No1200

Far left, the test station has an industrial character appropriate to the business of drilling and practical experiment.
Left, a ground floor passageway and a laboratory in the reception building; practical testing has now largely given way to computer-based research programmes.

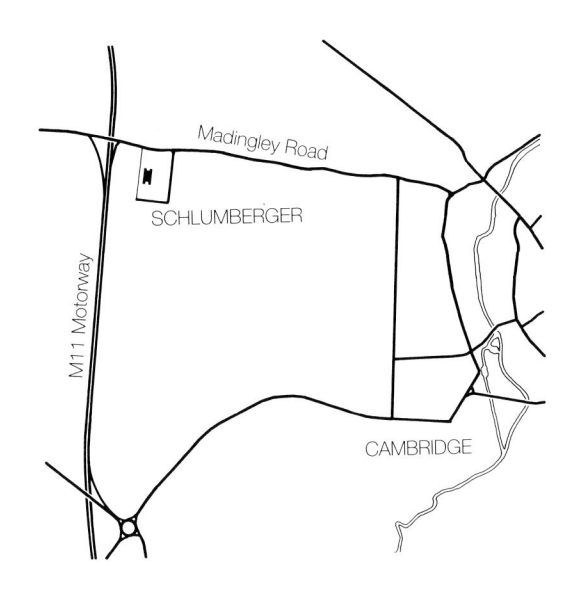

Location plan
1. British Antarctic Survey
2. storm water balancing pond
3. service yard, substations and mud tank
4. Schlumberger Cambridge Research: test station building
5. reception building
6. car parking
7. Computer-Aided Design Centre
8. School of Veterinary Medicine

Drawings

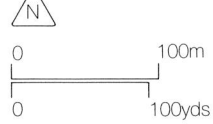

Ground floor and first floor plans with east–west cross-section through entrance hall

1 rock physics laboratory
2 scientist's room
3 WCs
4 discussion area
5 service yard
6 bridge in front of service entrance
7 double-height workshop
8 access tunnel
9 drilling mechanics laboratory
10 flow loop pit
11 underground high-pressure pump chamber
12 drilling pits
13 fluid mechanics laboratory
14 drilling test station
15 wellbore physics laboratory
16 kitchen
17 restaurant
18 winter garden
19 archive
20 library
21 laboratory
22 seismic laboratory
23 plant
24 meeting room
25 entrance hall
26 rheology laboratory
27 main entrance and terrace
28 conference room
29 teaching wall
30 bridge above entrance hall
31 computer room

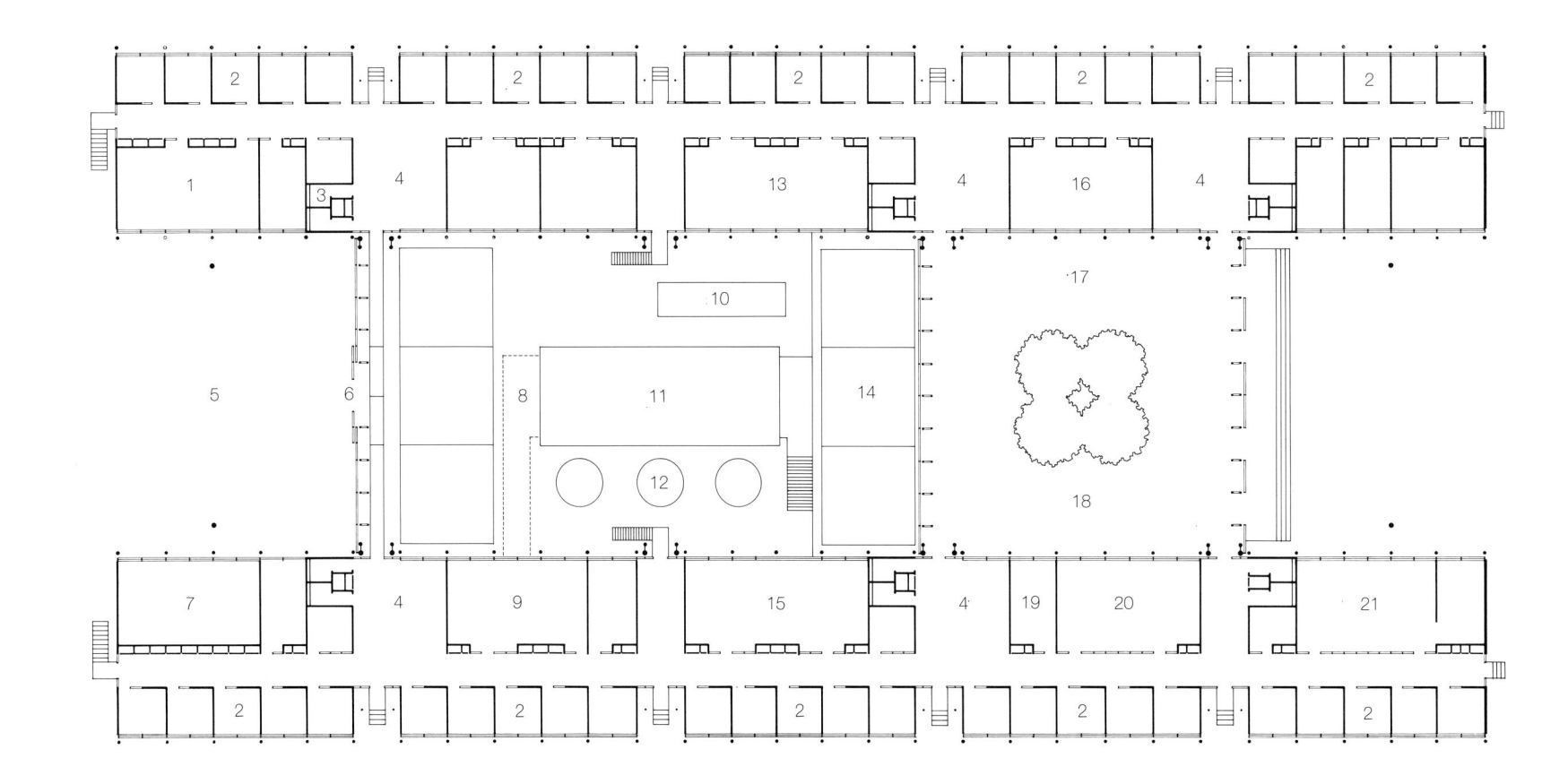

Test station building, ground floor plan

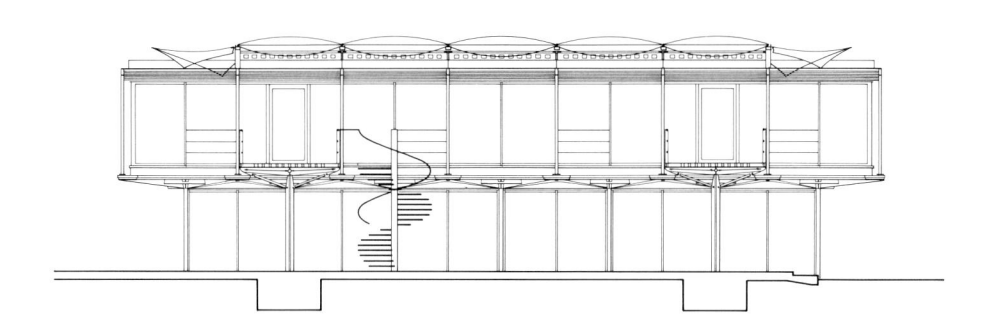

North–south cross-section through entrance hall

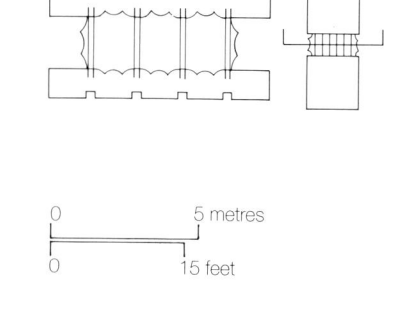

0 — 5 metres
0 — 15 feet

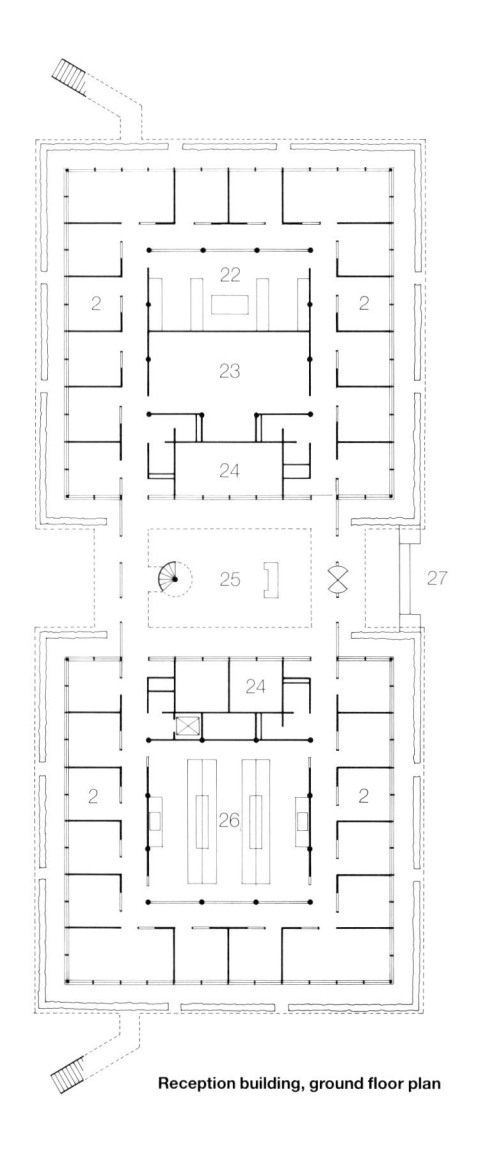

Reception building, ground floor plan

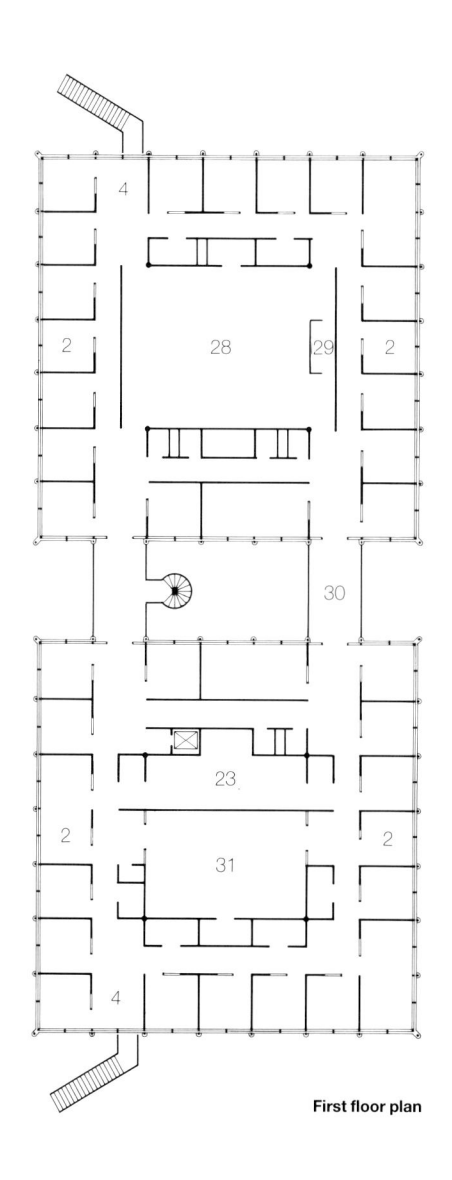

First floor plan

Detail sections through air-filled cushion roof above entrance hall

1. 1mm thick single layer polymeric membrane dressed up preformed flashing
2. 95mm thick rigid insulation
3. vapour barrier
4. 140mm deep ceiling panel: 15mm plywood, 50mm insulation, 125mm softwood frame
5. 15mm plywood underside of ceiling panel
6. polymeric membrane adhered to flashing
7. air feed pipe
8. stainless steel ventilator actuator
9. 6mm thick moveable transparent polycarbonate sheet with ventilation holes
10. 250mm high polyester powder-coated aluminium fascia
11. fixing bracket
12. 85 x 50 x 6mm galvanized steel cleat welded to top flange of beam
13. aluminium weather angle
14. 359 x 172mm UB
15. aluminium sliding door assembly
16. 50 x 30mm softwood packer
17. electrical conductor
18. three-layered ETFE film air-filled cushion; 65% silver dot matrix on underside of top sheet
19. 100 x 65 x 10mm RSA
20. 200 x 100 x 12mm RSA with ventilation slots
21. 7 x 6mm continuous brush round openings
22. 10mm thick ms plate to casting connector plate bolted between back to back 200 x 100 x 12mm RSAs
23. 5mm slip membrane
24. spheroidal graphite iron perimeter node casting
25. 89mm diameter CHS perimeter column
26. electrically-operated blind
27. thermally broken aluminium extrusion
28. zip-up gasket
29. air transfer plenum
30. single-ply polymeric membrane
31. 160 x 80 x 10mm RHS
32. 80 x 50 x 10mm ms flat
33. 200 x 100 x 12mm RSA
34. mill finished aluminium clamp
35. stainless steel wires at 250mm centres
36. ventilation
37. profiled metal flashing sealed to 5mm ms flat upstand
38. 100 x 75 x 12mm RSA
39. 10mm thick ms plate welded to 25mm base plate
40. 50 x 30mm stainless steel channel bracket
41. 12mm thick clear toughened glass
42. 12mm D shackle
43. welded ms lug
44. 180mm U bolt
45. canopy fabric

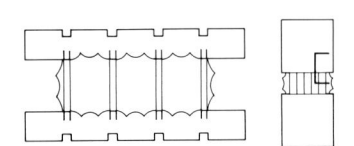

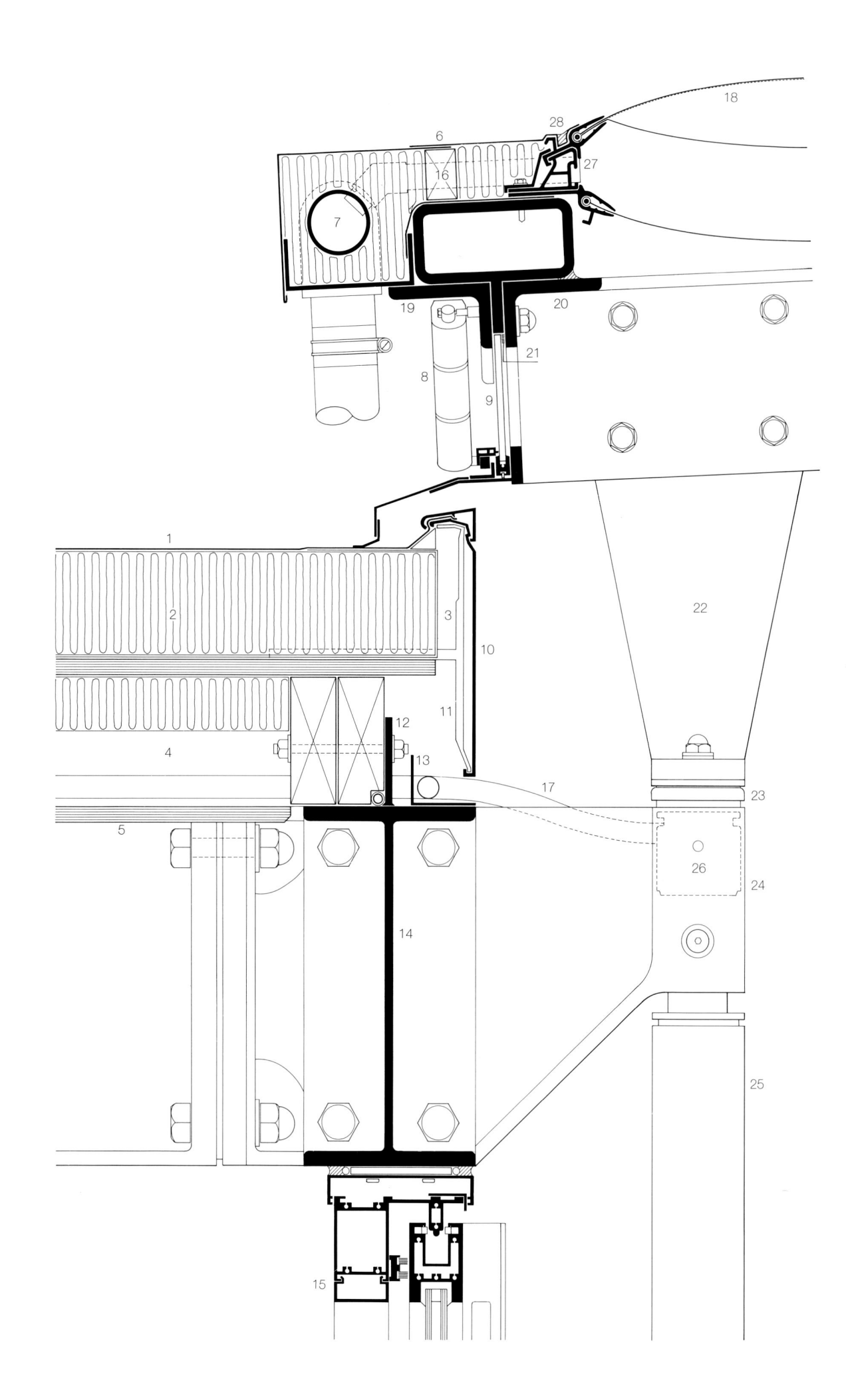

East–west cross-section through laboratories and scientists' rooms

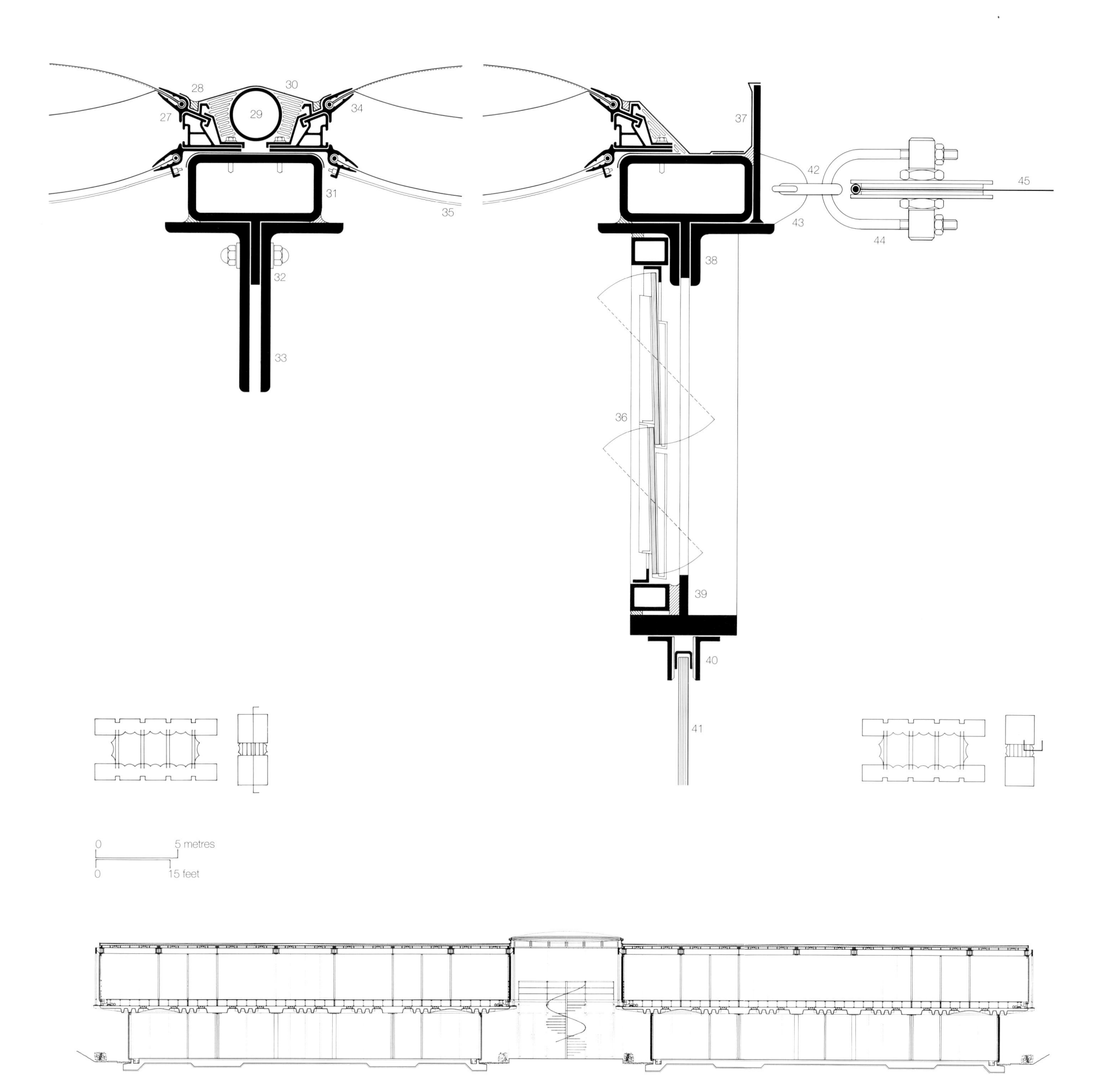

North–south long section through test station and winter garden

1 service yard
2 test station
3 flow loop
4 drilling test pit
5 plant rooms and services distribution
6 winter garden

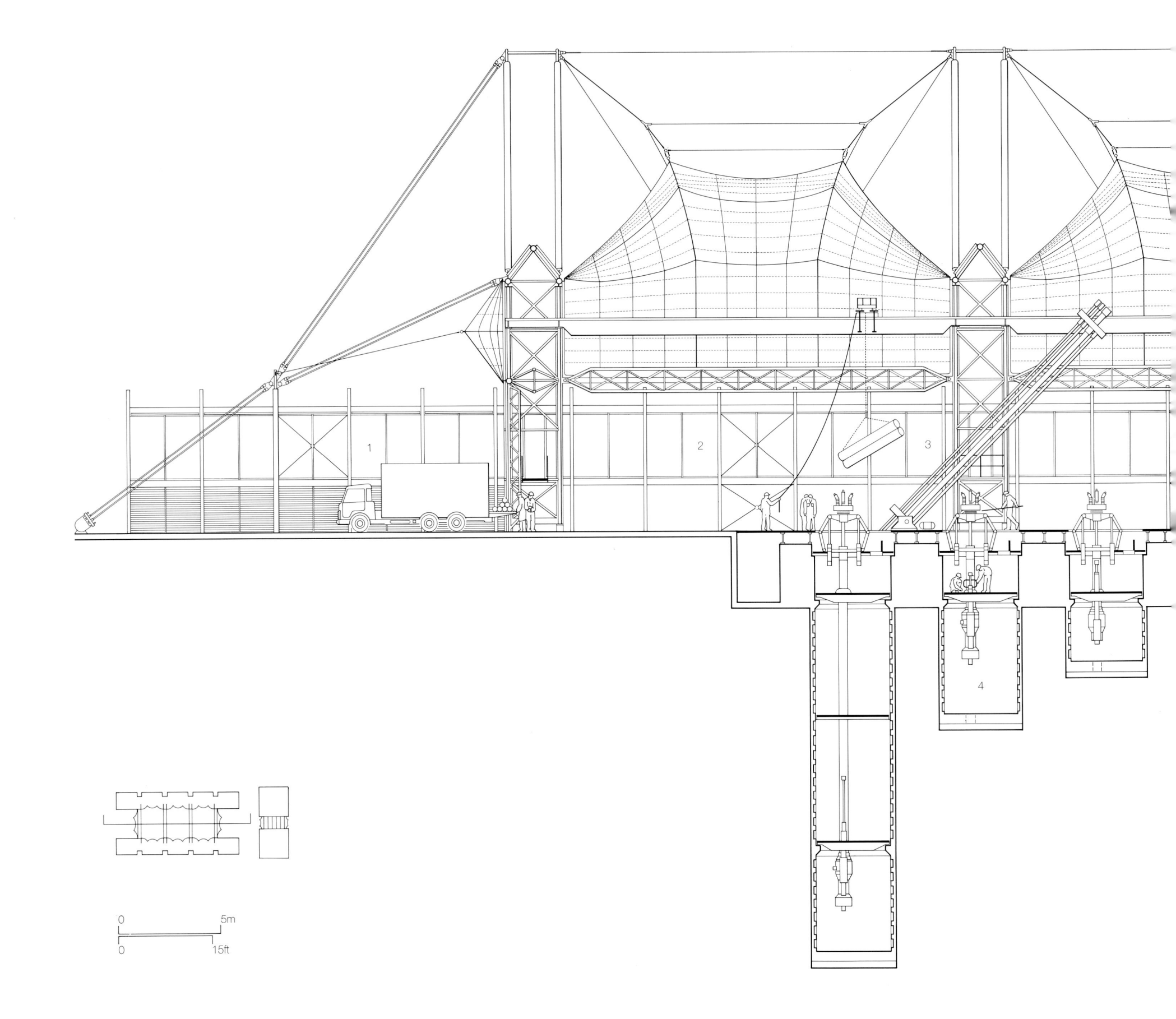

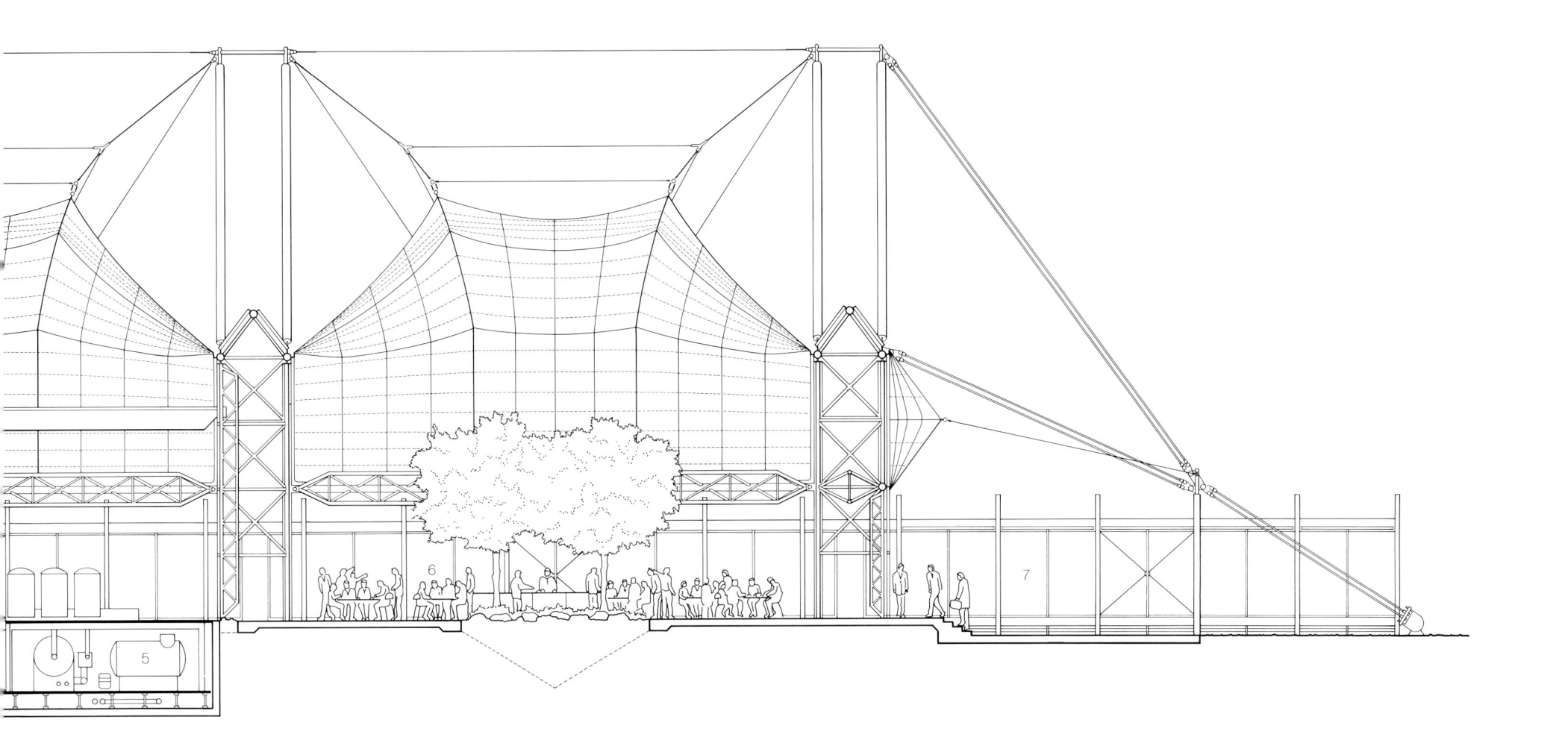

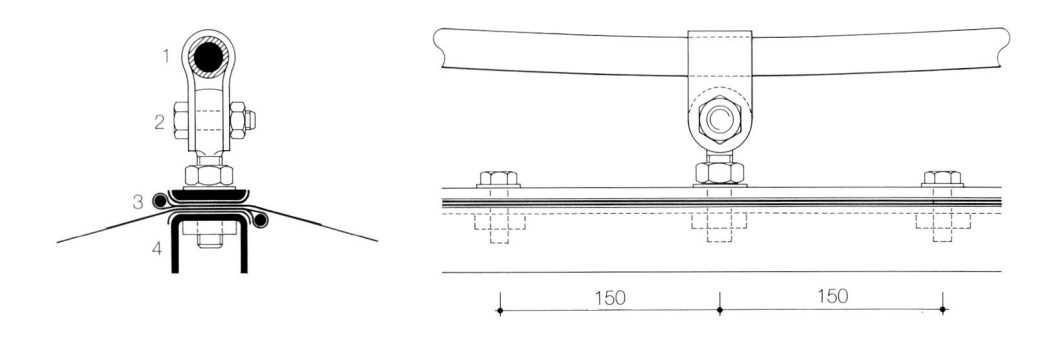

Detail of membrane ridge cable

1. 18mm diameter steel ridge cable, polypropylene mantled black
2. cable clamp at 750mm centres
3. roof membrane reinforced with 8mm steel cable at clamped edges
4. 50 x 40 x 4mm channel, polyester powder-coated white

East–west cross-section through test station
1. office and laboratory accommodation
2. plant rooms and services distribution
3. test station
4. flow loop pit
5. high-pressure pump chamber
6. drilling test pit

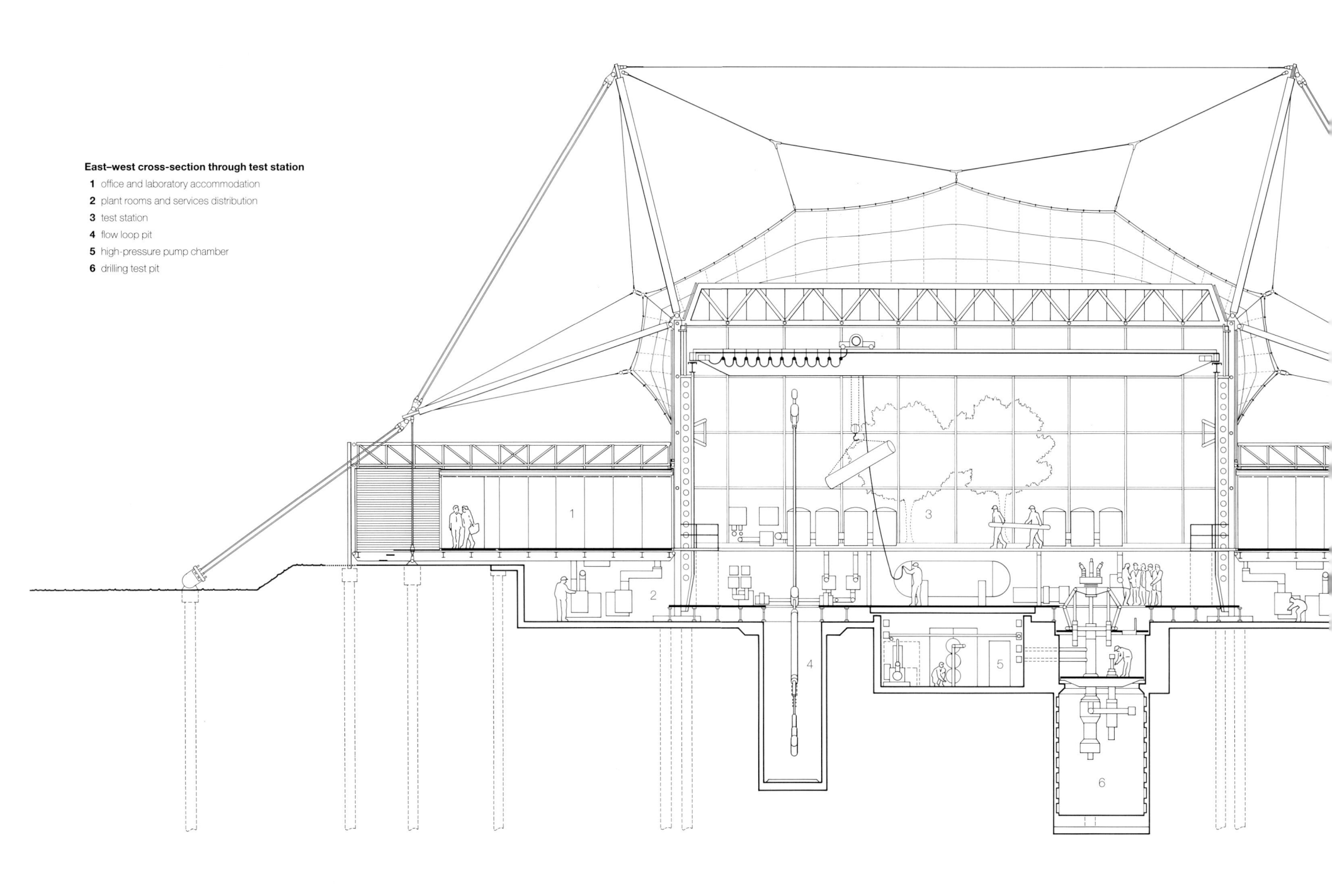

Detail of central ridge cable node-point assembly

1. 26mm diameter aerial cross tie cable
2. two-part cast steel node connector
3. 36mm diameter aerial cable with polypropylene sleeve
4. M33 threaded steel turnbuckle
5. two-part cast steel node connector
6. membrane ridge cable pick-up assembly
7. translucent PTFE-coated glass fibre membrane

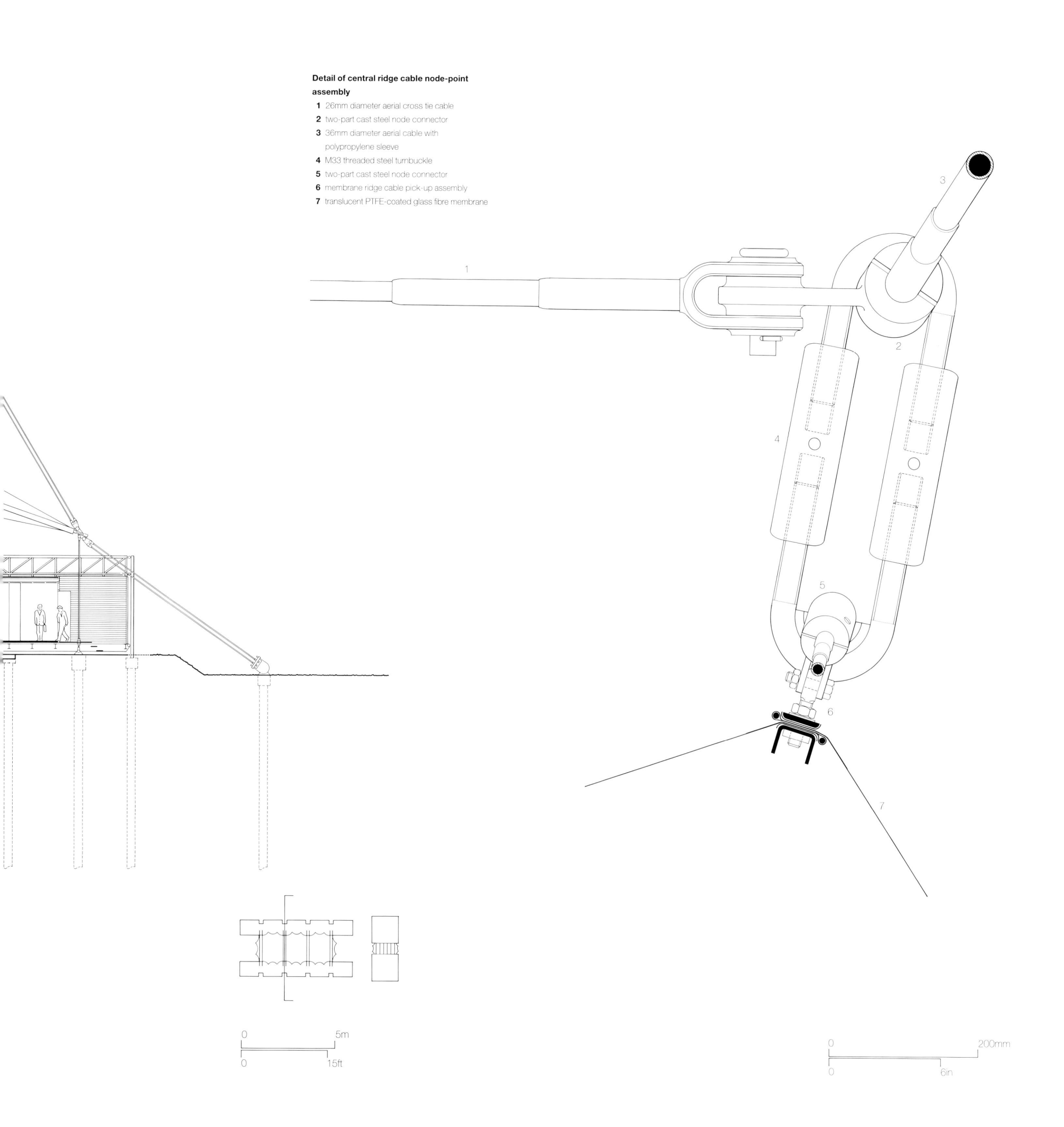

0   2m
0   6ft

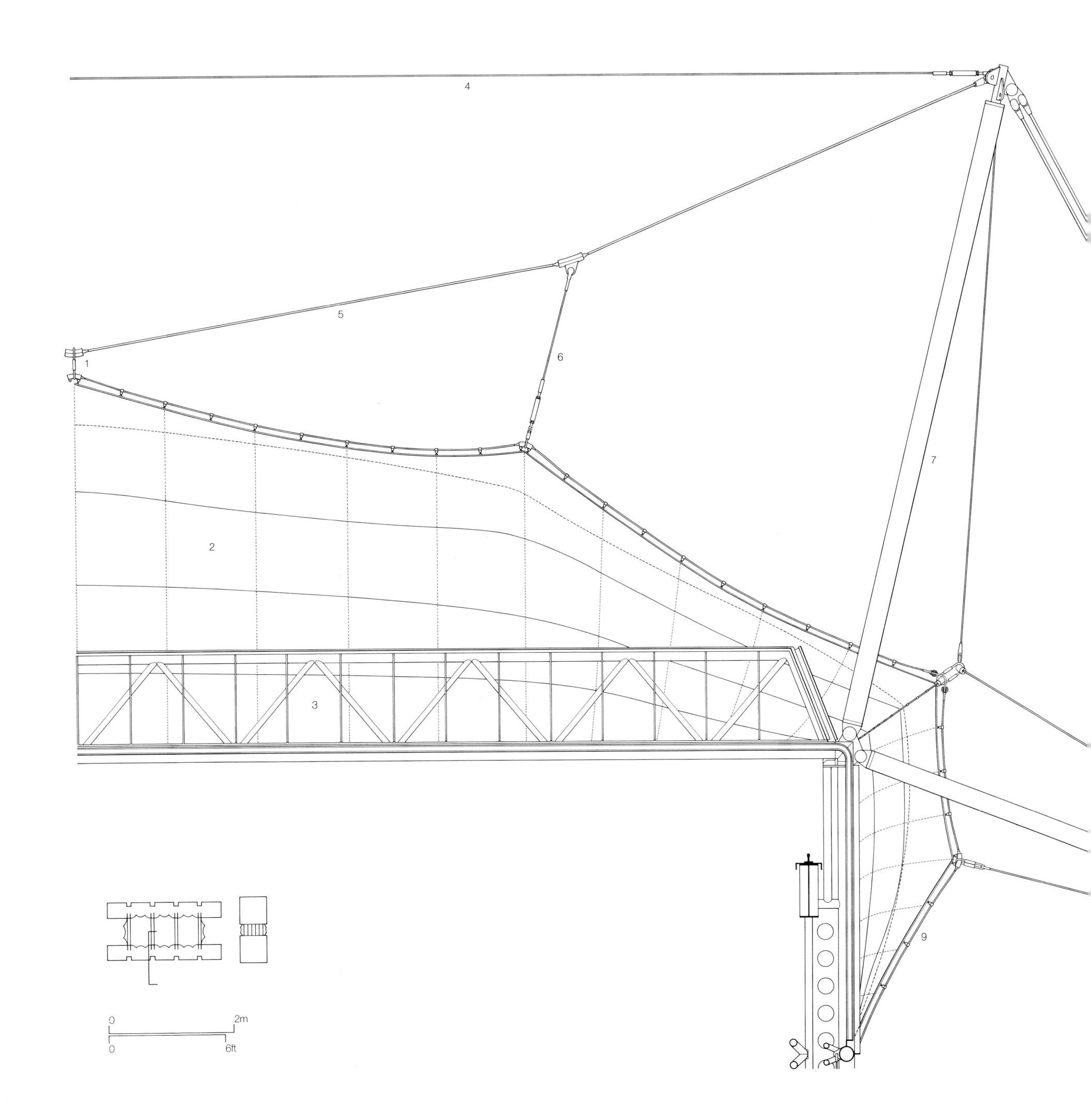

Sectional elevation of membrane roof support structure
1 ridge cable node-point
2 translucent PTFE-coated glass fibre membrane
3 patent glazed prismatic roof structure
4 26mm diameter boom cable
5 36mm diameter aerial cable
6 18mm diameter aerial hanger
7 328 x 8mm CHS upper boom and 273 x 8mm lower boom; stainless steel pin connection to steel lug welded to mast
8 26mm diameter eaves aerial cable
9 14mm diameter wall ridge cable
10 50mm diameter solid rods; cast steel spade connections and mounting plate connected by stainless steel pin to steel lug welded to boom ends

Projected section through junction between test station and laboratory block

1 membrane roof support structure: 328 x 8mm CHS upper boom and 273 x 8mm lower boom, connected by stainless steel pin to steel lug welded to mast
2 fixed and pneumatically controlled opening patent glazing above prismatic roof truss structure
3 solid steel tie bar, 30mm diameter
4 preformed clear polycarbonate sheet closer fixed to steelwork
5 anodized aluminium-framed single patent glazing, with 6mm thick clear float glass, fixed to steel lugs welded to mast
6 gantry crane girder and track
7 translucent PTFE-coated woven glass fibre membrane clamped to primary steelwork, with polypropylene mantled 16mm diameter steel ridge cables
8 membrane fixing member spanning between towers; 100mm equal angle and 100 x 8mm steel plate fin continuously welded to 220 x 8mm CHS tube
9 anodized aluminium-framed single clerestory glazing with 6mm thick clear float glass
10 sliding rubber seal to allow differential movement
11 pressed steel closer panel
12 external roof truss to laboratory block; 114 x 5mm CHS upper boom and 76 x 4mm CHS lower boom, connected by stainless steel pin to steel lugs welded to 139 x 8mm CHS column. Purlin connections suspended below
13 built-up roof construction achieving a U-value of 0.22 W/m²/°C. See following page for details
14 perforated steel acoustic ceiling tiles with stoved alkyd finish
15 polyester powder-coated aluminium fixed-framed perimeter windows; glazed with 21mm thick laminated clear glass
16 built-up floor construction achieving a U-value of 0.45 W/m²/°C. See following page for details
17 power, data and telecommunications cabling distributed along troughs in floor decking; rising within partition walls to outlets
18 heating and ventilating services distributed from undercroft
19 test station floor: raised extruded aluminium decking with punched holes
20 concrete pile caps
21 reinforced concrete ground slab, 250mm thick

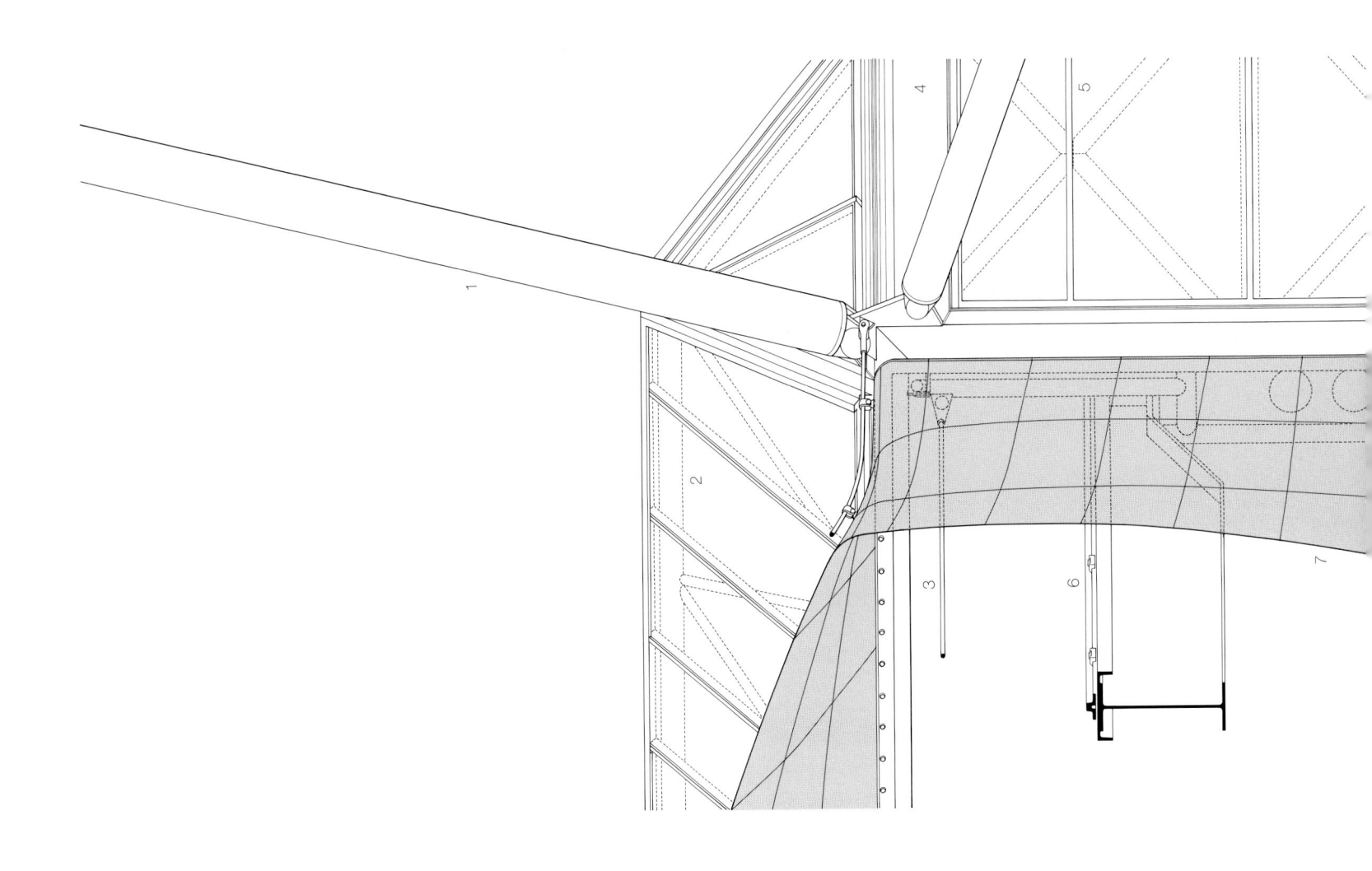

2m / 6ft

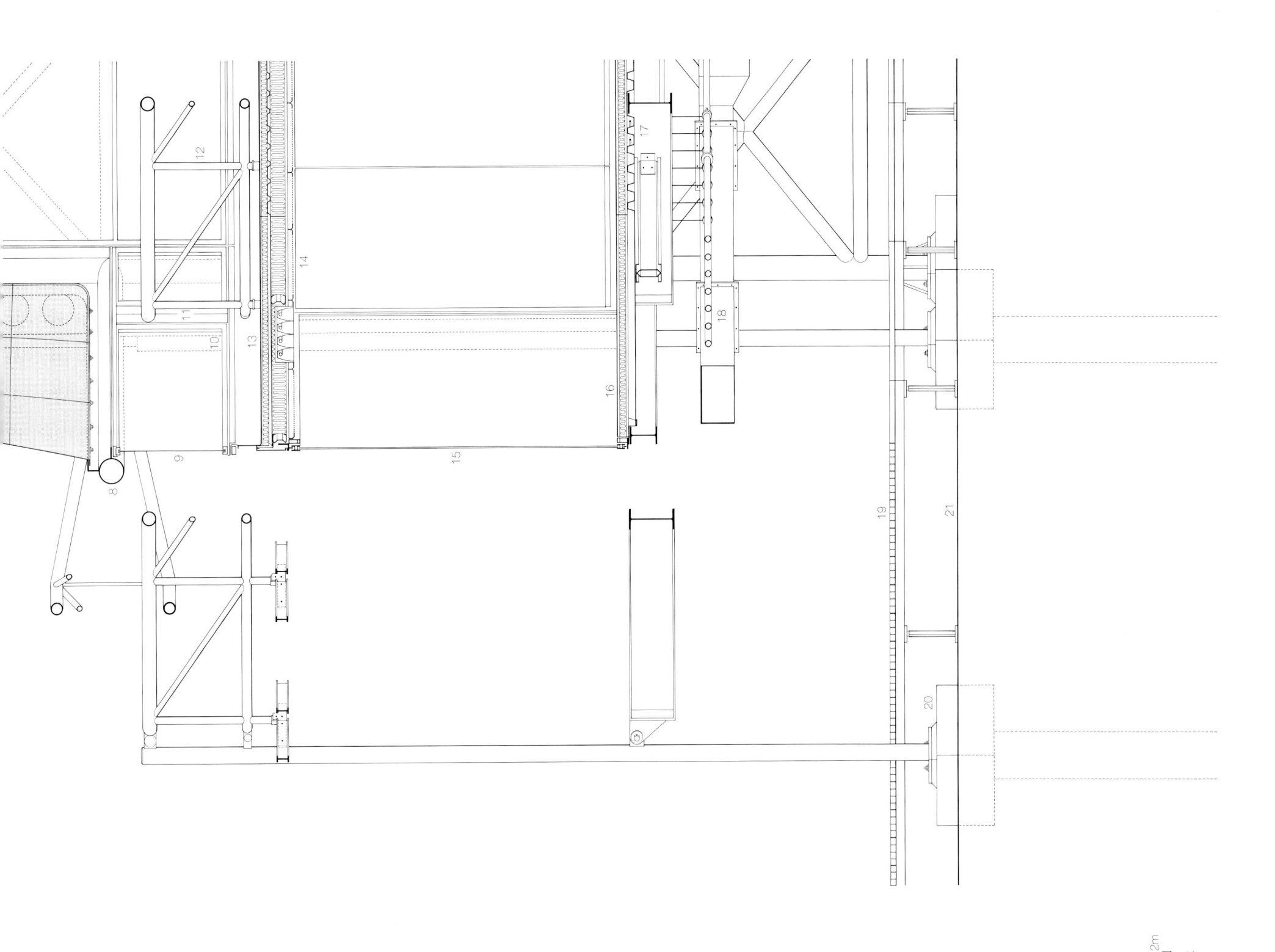

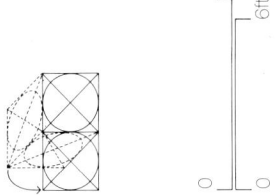

Detailed section through perimeter of laboratory block and test station

1 translucent PTFE-coated woven glass fibre membrane roof with 8mm polypropylene mantled steel cable reinforcement at perimeter and lap joints; 50 x 4mm mild steel channel and 50 x 6mm ms plate clamping members at ridges with white PVC isolating strips to protect fabric; stainless steel M16 bolts at 150mm centres; all steel parts polyester powder-coated white

2 membrane fixing clamp: 50 x 6mm steel plate strip; M16 bolts at 150mm centres; white PVC isolating strips

3 membrane fixing member spanning between towers; 100mm equal angle and 100 x 8mm steel plate fin continuously welded to 220 x 8mm CHS tube

4 anticipated movement envelope at perimeter + 10mm vertical + 40mm horizontal

5 extruded aluminium glazing retaining channel with solid rubber seal to allow differential and rotational movement

6 anodized aluminium-framed single-glazed clerestory; 6mm thick clear float glass

7 frame bedded on 10mm thick semi-rigid rubber seal to allow differential and rotational movement

8 139 x 8mm CHS column

9 laboratory/office roof truss; upper boom 114 x 5mm CHS, lower boom 76 x 4mm CHS; stainless steel pin connections to steel lugs welded to CHS column; purlin connections suspended below

10 continuous pressed anodized aluminium flashing

11 90 x 50 x 5mm RHS clerestory glazing support member welded to laboratory/ office truss structure

12 preformed polymeric cloak and membrane soaker fixed round purlin hangers with stainless steel clips

13 roof build-up: 1mm thick single layer polymeric membrane; dressed up preformed purlin connector flashing; expanded poly-styrene insulation preformed to falls on 25mm deep profiled galvanized steel decking

14 extruded aluminium fascia panel, polyester powder-coated dark grey

15 continuous 100 x 75mm galvanized steel angle for glazing fixing bolted to purlin hanger

16 114 x 73mm cold formed galvanized steel purlin

17 100mm thick mineral fibre insulation suspended from roof deck

18 polythene vapour barrier

19 600 x 600mm perforated steel acoustic ceiling tiles in concealed fixing system with stoved alkyd finish

20 extruded aluminium window framing section, polyester powder-coated dark grey

21 21mm thick laminated clear glass

22 fan-assisted low pressure hot water convector at perimeter

23 studded rubber flooring on 22mm thick tongued and grooved chipboard; 60mm thick expanded poly-styrene insulation; 22mm chipboard

24 70mm deep profiled galvanized steel decking

25 254 x 146 x 31 kg/m galvanized steel UB edge beam

26 406 x 178 x 74 kg/m galvanized steel primary beam

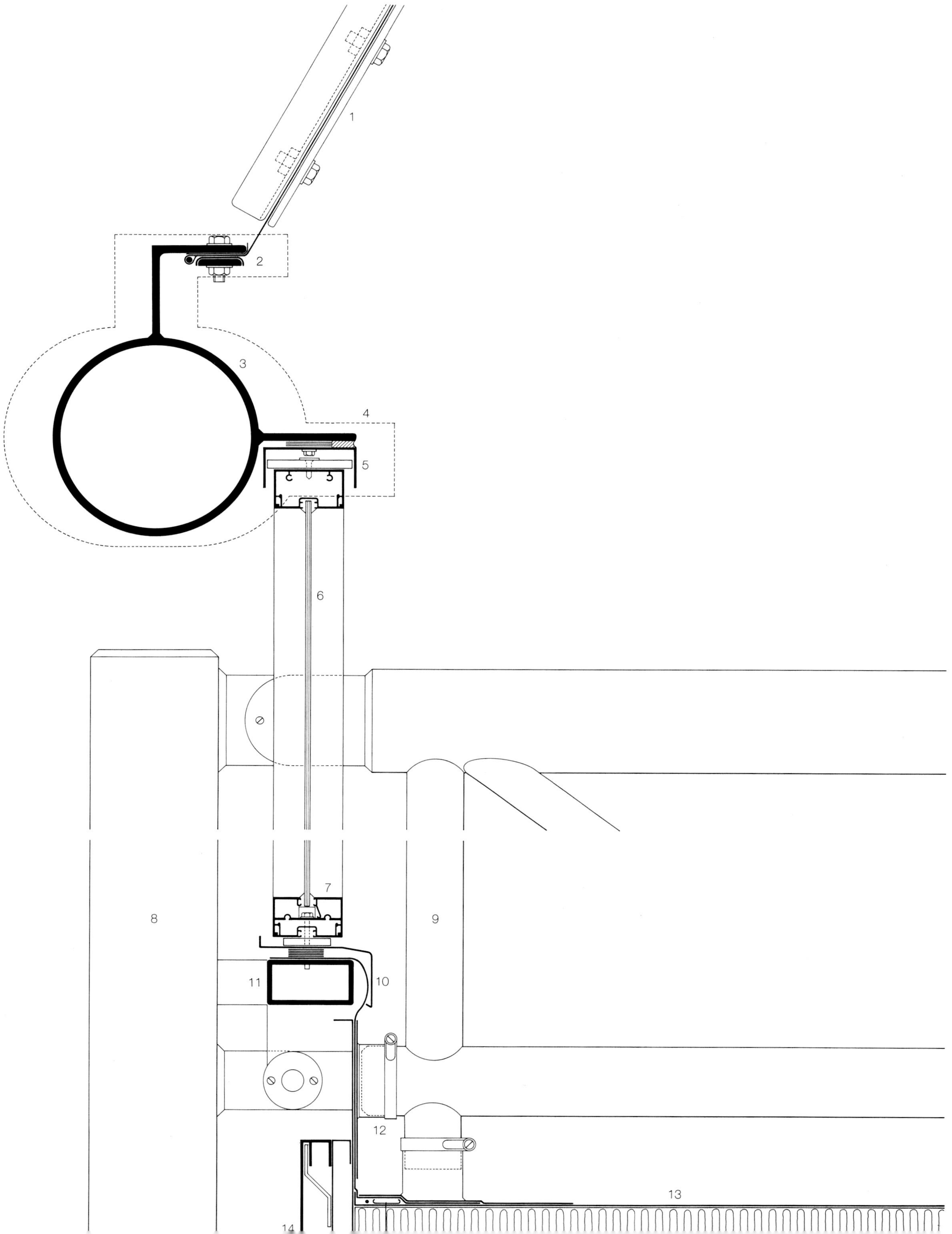

2906

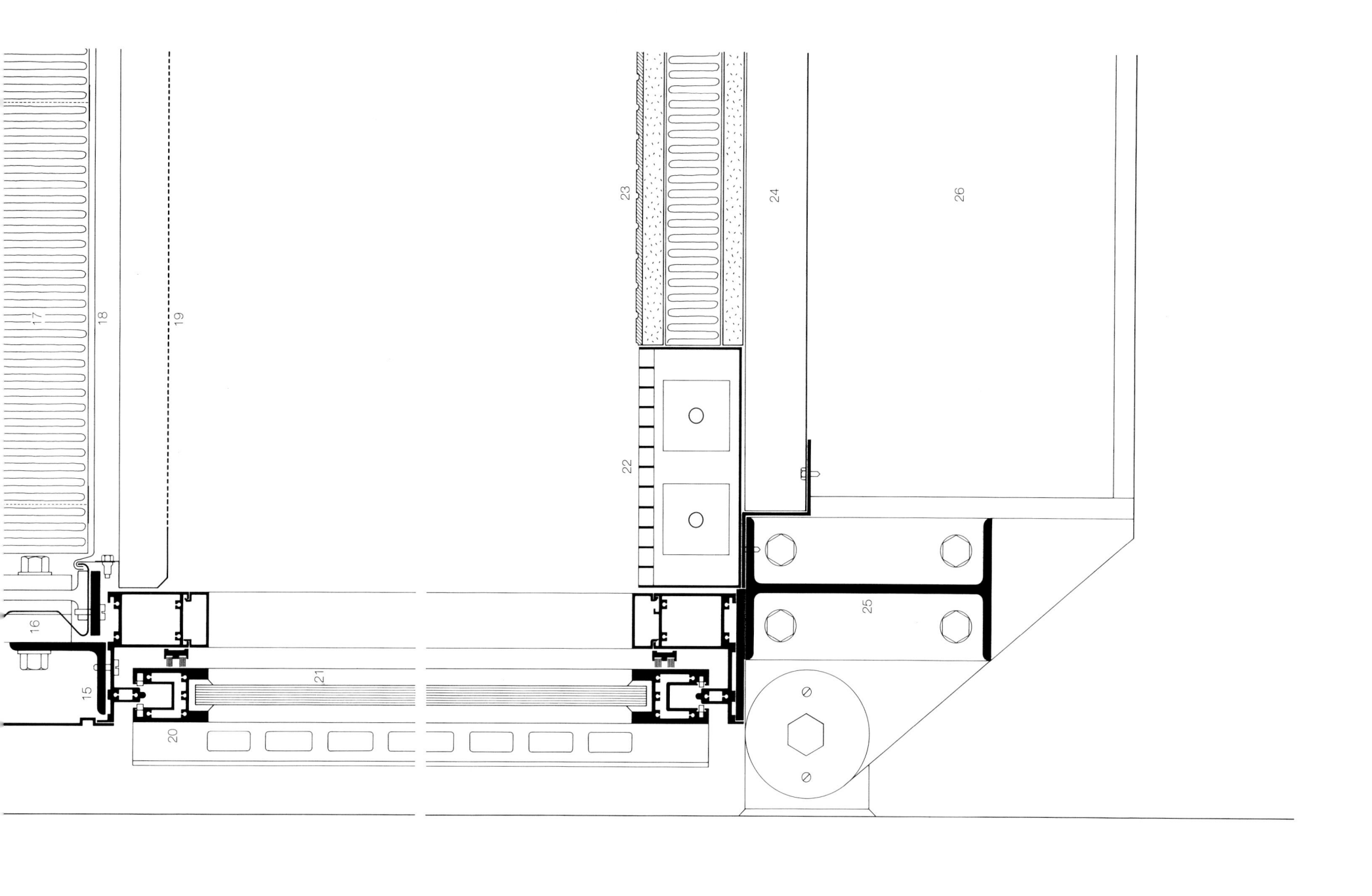

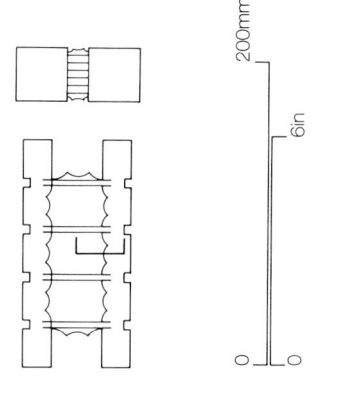

200mm
6in

Detailed section through perimeter of scientists' offices

1. laboratory/office roof truss: upper boom 114 x 5mm CHS, lower boom 76 x 4mm CHS; stainless steel pin connections to steel lugs welded to CHS column; purlin connections suspended below
2. 139 x 8mm CHS column
3. preformed polymeric cloak and membrane soaker fixed round purlin hangers with stainless steel clips
4. roof build-up: 1mm thick single layer polymeric membrane, dressed up preformed purlin connector flashing; expanded polystyrene insulation preformed to falls on 25mm deep profiled galvanized steel decking
5. extruded aluminium fascia panel, polyester powder-coated dark grey
6. continuous 100 x 75mm galvanized steel angle for glazing fixing, bolted to purlin hanger
7. galvanized 114 x 73mm cold formed steel purlin
8. 100mm thick mineral fibre insulation suspended from roof deck
9. polythene vapour barrier
10. 600 x 600mm perforated steel acoustic ceiling tiles in concealed fixing system with stoved alkyd finish
11. double glazing: 6mm thick toughened clear glass; sealed glazing unit 24mm thick overall; U-value 2.8 W/m²°C
12. extruded aluminium sliding window framing section, polyester powder-coated dark grey
13. extruded aluminium head box for electrically controlled external blinds, spanning 3.6m between plate steel lugs welded to CHS column; polyester powder-coated dark grey
14. 80mm wide pressed aluminium sun screen louvres, polyester powder-coated dark grey; 4mm diameter stainless steel guide cables; 10mm thick steel base plate, polyester powder-coated dark grey
15. T-section fixing plate bolted to steel lug welded to CHS column
16. 18mm diameter steel cross bracing rods with solid steel anchor plates; located at five bay intervals along laboratory/office block perimeter
17. fan-assisted low pressure hot water convector at perimeter
18. carpet tiles on 22mm thick tongued and grooved chipboard; 60mm thick expanded polystyrene insulation; 22mm chipboard
19. 70mm deep profiled galvanized steel decking
20. 254 x 146 x 31 kg/m galvanized steel UB edge beam
21. 406 x 178 x 74 kg/m galvanized steel primary beam
22. reinforced concrete blinding and kerb upstand
23. extruded aluminium louvres in aluminium frame with bird/vermin screen on inside face; polyester powder-coated dark grey
24. crushed stone surround

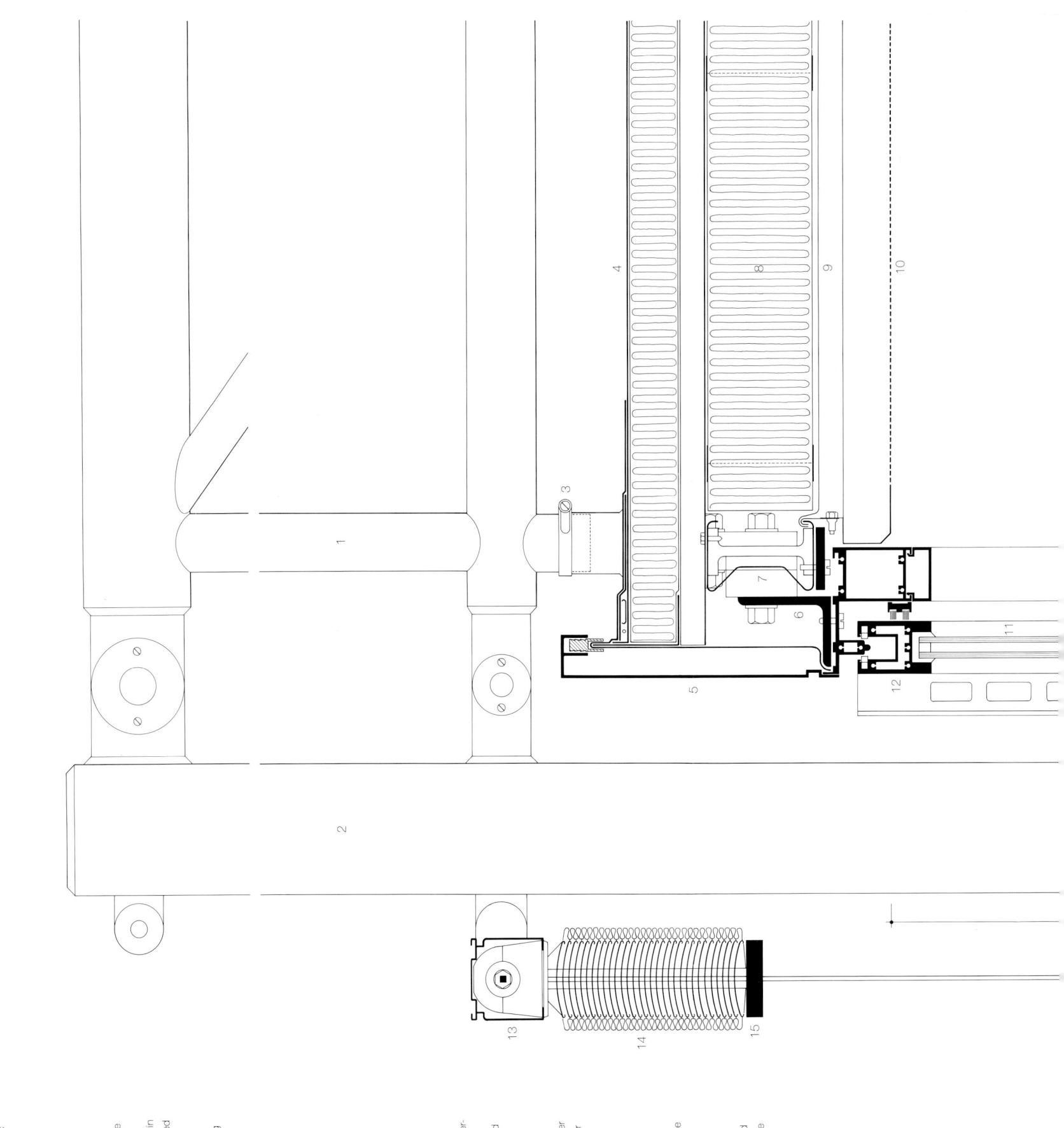

200mm
6in

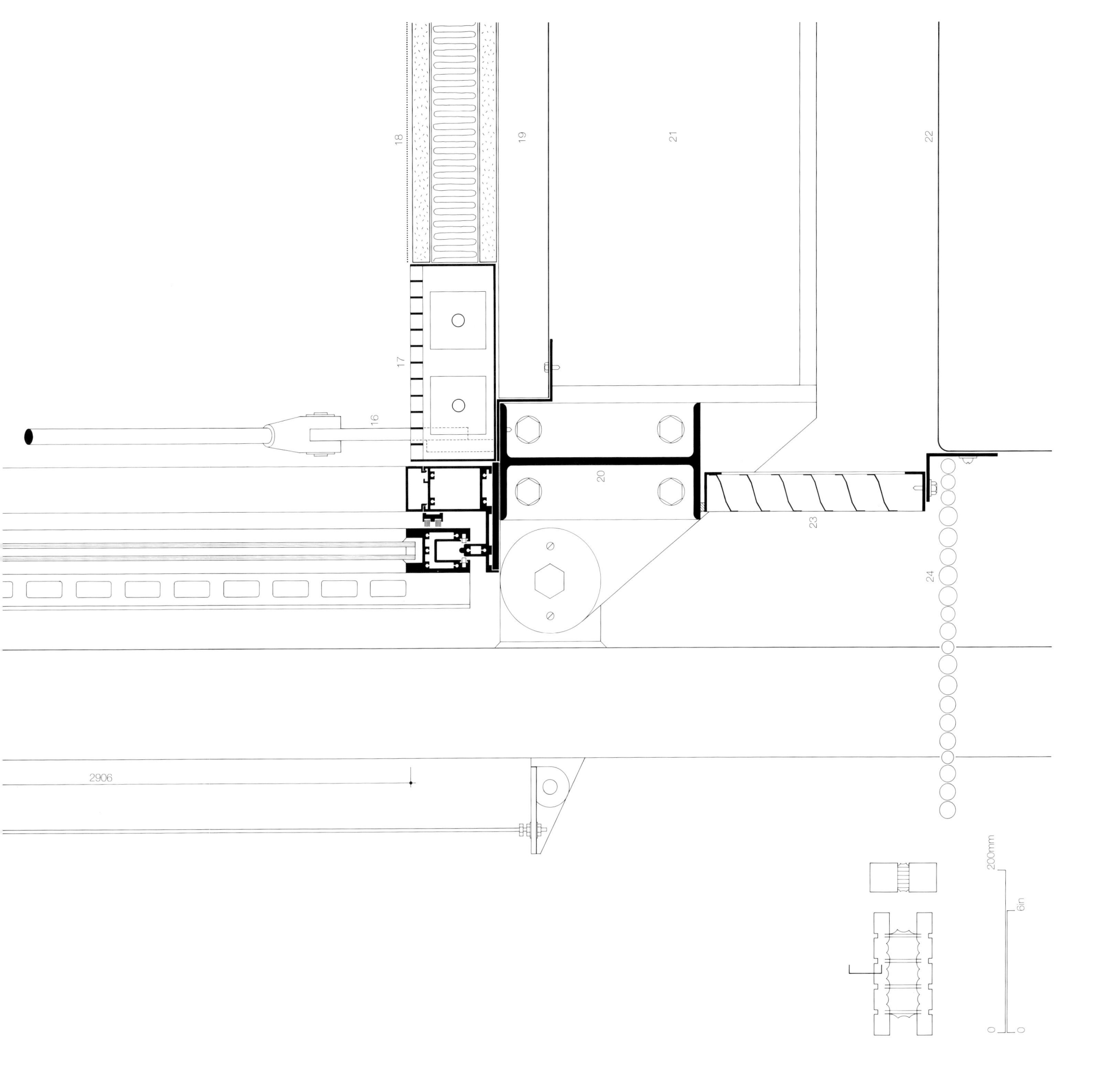

Notes

1. The development of the IBM Pilot Head Office project is discussed in depth by Graham Vickers in *Norman Foster, Team 4 and Foster Associates: Buildings and Projects, Volume 1 1964–73*, Watermark Press, London and Hong Kong, 1991, pp.128–43.
2. Ibid. The long gestation of the German Car Centre project is related by David Jenkins, pp.216–19.
3. Ibid. Ehrenkrantz's influence on Foster Associates is outlined by David Jenkins, pp.100–105 and Frank Duffy, pp.182–87.
4. For more information see *Mound Stand, Lord's Cricket Ground* by David Jenkins, Architecture in Detail, Phaidon Press Limited, London, 1991.
5. Further technical detail on the history and development of fabric membrane enclosures is contained in an article by Brian Forster of Ove Arup & Partners, published in the *Arup Journal*, Autumn 1985.
6. Mies' address to the IIT is reprinted in *Mies van der Rohe* by Philip Johnson, Secker & Warburg, London, 1978, pp.203–4.

Selected published articles

Building, 10 June 1983
The Architectural Review, May 1984; Colin Davies
Architects' Journal, 1 February 1984; Birkin Haward
Architects' Journal, 24 October 1984;
  Henry Herzberg
Architecture d'Aujourdhui, February 1985
Architects' Journal, 15 May 1985; Patrick Hannay
Architects' Journal, 18 September 1985;
  Steven Groak
Blueprint, July 1986; Rowan Moore
Architecture + Urbanism, September 1986
Country Life, 17 November 1988; Ken Powell
Architects' Journal, 28 October 1992; John Winter

Chronology

Spring 1982
Twenty practices interviewed by Schlumberger
April 1982
Preliminary project appraisal presented to Schlumberger by Michael Hopkins and Partners
29 August 1983
Contract start date
21 September 1984
Scheduled contract completion date
November 1984
Main contract works completed
November 1984
Scheduled building occupation date
Spring 1985
Test station building occupied and test station in use
September 1990
Michael Hopkins and Partners briefed by Schlumberger for new reception building
December 1990/January 1991
Project presentation to Schlumberger
April 1991
Management contractor appointed
7 August 1991
Contract start date
24 August 1992
Main contract works complete, building occupied
19 November 1992
Reception building officially opened

Architects and Consultants

Test Station Building
Location Madingley Road, Cambridge
Client Schlumberger Cambridge Research Ltd
Architects Michael Hopkins and Partners
Design Team Michael Hopkins, John Pringle, Chris Williamson, Nic Bewick, Robin Snell, John Eger
Quantity Surveyors White & Turner; Roger White
Structural Engineers Anthony Hunt Associates; Anthony Hunt, Alan Jones, Bob Barton
Structural Engineers: Membrane and Cables Ove Arup & Partners Lightweight Structures Group; Brian Forster, Alastair Day, Tristram Carfrae
Services Engineers YRM Engineers; Steve Green, Richard Windmill, Mike Kings
Acoustic Consultant Tim Smith Acoustics
Test Rig Design and Commissioning Vickers Design & Projects
Main Contractor Bovis Construction Ltd
Project Manager Bob Clarke

Reception Building
Architects Michael Hopkins and Partners
Design Team Michael Hopkins, John Pringle, James Greaves, Alan Jones, Annabel Hollick, Tom Emerson
Quantity Surveyors Davis Langdon & Everest; Ian Dyke, Clive Lewis, Michael Gildea
Structural Engineers Buro Happold (Leeds); Michael Dickson, Mick Green, Peter Moseley, Steve Gregson, Teresa Murphy
PVC Canopy Design Buro Happold (Bath)
Services Engineers Buro Happold; Peter Moseley, David Kingstone
Main Contractor Team Management (Southern)
Project Managers: John Coultier, Kevin Atkinson

Contractors and Suppliers

Test Station Building
Earthworks: Darby (Sutton) Ltd
Piling Simplex Piling Ltd
Reinforced Concrete May Gurney (Technical Services) Ltd; V.M. Donnelly & Sons Ltd
Structural Steelwork including Paintwork Blight & White Ltd
Membrane Roof Stromeyer Ingenieurbau GmbH
Test Station Glazing Frederick Sage & Co. Ltd
Office/Laboratory Glazing Alifabs (Contracts) Ltd
Acoustic Glass Walls Alcan Windows Ltd
Flat Roofs, Solid Walls, Floordecking R.M. Douglas Roofing Ltd
Stairs, Sundry Metalwork, Floor Gratings and Loading Bay Door Non-Corrosive Metal Products Ltd
Gantry Cranes Allen Cranes (Northampton) Ltd
Pre-Cast Concrete Units Trent Concrete Structures Ltd
Mechanical and Electrical Services Norstead Engineering Services Ltd
Suspended Ceilings and Partitions Classtech Ltd
Suspended Floor SOL Construction Ltd
External Louvres Environmental Technology Ltd
Computer Floor System Floors (UK) Ltd
Carpets Derry Treanor Ltd
Rubber Flooring Variety Floors Ltd
Fire Protection Fylde Fire Precautions Ltd
High Voltage Switchgear Enclosure Wyseplan Ltd
High Voltage Switchgear Electrical Installations Ltd
Roller Shutter Brady Doors Ltd
Suppliers/Manufacturers of Roof Membrane Material Verseidag Industrietextilen GmbH
Roof Cables Pfeifer Seil und Hebetechnik GmbH
Steelwork British Steel Corporation
Solid Rods Reinforcement Steel Services Ltd
Steelwork Inspection Messrs Sandberg
Paint United Paint Co.
Flat Roof Membrane Sarna (UK) Ltd
Flat Roof/Floor Decks Precision Metal Forming Ltd
Solid Wall Cladding Plannja Dobel Ltd
Flat Roof Insulation Vencel Resil Ltd
Office/Laboratory Glazing Schuco; Heinz Schurmann GmbH & Co.
Roof Glazing Vitral International A/S
Test Station Glazing A/S Raufoss Ammunisjonsfabrikker
Acoustic Glass Alcan Safety Glass Ltd; Plyglass Ltd
Opaque Acoustic Glass Doulton Glass Industries Ltd
Partitions, Cupboards, Shelving Tecno SpA
Ceilings Thermo Acoustic Products Ltd
Double Glazed Units Pilkington Glass Ltd
Opaque Glass Multiglass Ltd
Floor Insulation Dow Chemical Co. Ltd
Carpet Desso (UK) Ltd
Rubber Flooring Harefield Rubber Co. Ltd
Winter Garden Paving Empire Stone Co. Ltd
High Voltage Switchgear GEC Distribution Switchgear Ltd
Fire Protection Mandoval Ltd
Office Heaters F.H. Biddle Ltd
Winter Garden Heaters Powrmatic Ltd
Office Lighting AEG Telefunken (UK) Ltd
Test Station Lighting Franz Sill GmbH
Floor Grilles Air Diffusion Ltd
Fire Alarms Chubb Fire Security Ltd
Drainage Channels ACO Ltd
Electrical Floor Outlets Van Geel Systems Ltd
Sanitary Fittings Ceramica Dolomite SpA; Armitage Shanks
Taps Ideal Standard Ltd
Showers Aqualisa Products Ltd
Sundry Metalwork BR (UK) Ltd
Ironmongery Elementer Industrial Design Ltd

Reception Building
Ground Works John Doyle Construction
Ground Floor Columns Britannia Fabrications
Fire Protection Mebon Ltd
Permanent Formwork Ferro-Monk Systems
First Floor Slab Intex Builders
Structural Steelwork Tubeworkers Ltd
Cladding Ebor Aluminium Systems
Roof Infill Panels Kingston Craftsmen Structural Timber Engineering
Roof Membrane Permanite (Cambridge Asphalte Co.)
Mechanical Services Aqua Mechanical Services
Electrical Services Macmillan & Co. (Electrical Engineers)
Partitions Tecno UK
Raised Floor Unilock Access Floors
External Blinds Unilock HCP
Entrance Hall Steelwork & Canopies Sheetfabs (Nottingham)
Decorating Simpson Hall
Lift Gough & Co. (Hanley)
Entrance Hall Glazing Marcus Summers
Spiral Staircase Cornish Stairways
Carpet Milliken Contract Carpets
Metalwork Ferguson Engineering
Landscaping Landstructure Ltd
Cladding Supplier Schuco International
Glass Block Panels Bouwmag
Foil Cushion Vector
Paving Empire Stone